He is altogether lovely

Discovering Christ in the Song of Solomon

Roger Ellsworth

 EVANGELICAL PRESS

EVANGELICAL PRESS
Grange Close, Faverdale North Industrial Estate, Darlington,
Co. Durham, DL3 0PH, England

First published 1998

British Library Cataloguing in Publication Data available

ISBN 0 85234 406 6

Printed and bound in Great Britain by Creative Print and Design
Wales, Ebbw Vale

For my good friends,
Gene and Dorothy Baker
and in memory of Immanuel's beloved deacon
and my friend,
Paul Grammer

'I thank my God upon every remembrance of you… '
(Phil. 1:3).

Contents

Conclusion

Foreword

Roger Ellsworth follows a long line of teachers who have expounded this most beautiful of songs in such a way as to show
the love that exists between the Lord and his people. Among
the early Christian writers and preachers to draw attention to
this spiritual meaning are Athanasius, Basil, Chrysostom and
Augustine. In the Middle Ages Bernard of Clairvaux not only
preached many sermons from this book but composed a poem
based on it, from which we have the well-known hymn 'Jesus,
the very thought of thee'. Luther lectured on the Song show-
ing how Solomon speaks for all his people who are the bride
of the Lord. The Puritans found great spiritual benefit from it
and James Durham wrote a helpful exposition that was
commended by John Owen. In the foreword to George
Burrowes' commentary on the Song of Songs, Dr Lloyd-Jones
commends among other things the way in which the author
helps Christians to appreciate the Song's spiritual treasures.
Spurgeon loved to preach Christ from this book and Hudson
Taylor's little study *Union and Communion* has become something of a classic.

This spiritual understanding of the Song has been out of
favour for much of the twentieth century and there seems to
be a growing number of evangelical scholars actively pushing

the natural interpretation and downplaying the spiritual. It certainly fits in with the present obsession with sex in our society and the low biblical spirituality found in Western Christianity.

We should remember that as Paul presents the teaching on husband-and-wife relationships he quotes Genesis 2:24: 'For this reason a man shall leave his father and mother and be joined to his wife, and the two shall become one flesh.' Immediately he adds, 'This is a great mystery; but I speak concerning Christ and the church' (Eph. 5:31-32). The mystery is the special marriage relationship between Christ and his church revealed in the gospel. This spiritual union between the Lord and his people is the model for human marriage. The earthly type leads the believer to consider the heavenly antitype. We have exactly the same position presented in the Old Testament — e.g. Isaiah 54:5-6; Jeremiah 2:1-3; 31:32; Ezekiel 16; 23; Hosea 1-3; Psalm 45. The last reference is the closest parallel to the Song that we have in the Bible. The title of the psalm makes it clear that it is a 'love song' and the contents suggest a royal marriage song. From this original context it was seen as a pointer to the ideal King (Messiah) and his people. Hebrews 1:8 leaves us in no doubt about its Messianic significance. In the same way, we are encouraged to take this best of all songs and look beyond the natural level to view Christ's loveliness and to be taken up with love for him.

The antidote to immoral premarital relationships and the breaking of marriage vows among professing Christians is not more sex and marriage manuals or counselling sessions but a return to our 'first love'. When Israel went away from God and served other gods they got involved in all kinds of immoral sexual practices. Through his prophets, God called out to his people to return: 'O Israel, return to the Lord your God... I will heal their backsliding, I will love them freely' (Hosea 14:1,4). In the New Testament the Lord calls the wayward churches to repent and do the first works. He also says, 'As many as I love, I rebuke and chasten... Behold I stand at the door and knock. If anyone hears my voice and opens the door, I will come in to him and dine with him, and he with me' (Rev. 2:4-5; 3:19-20).

You do not have to agree with every detail of the author's interpretation to benefit from this book. Because Mr Ellsworth knows his Bible well he will not lead you astray into a false spirituality or to unwholesome conclusions. In a warm and fresh way he brings you to Christ and to all the great doctrines of the Christian faith. The messages challenge the church of Jesus Christ and its individual members concerning their relationship to the Lord and their service for him.

I commend this valuable study and pray that it will result in an evangelical spiritual revival at a personal and church level.

Philip H. Eveson
London Theological Seminary
January 1998

Preface

The Song of Solomon has long been a love of mine, a love that I have desired to put into words with the hope that others might find something of the blessing this book has given me. These pages represent, all too faintly I fear, the fulfilment of that desire.

Much of what is found here was originally delivered in sermon form to my wonderful Immanuel family. Their enthusiasm for biblical preaching is a source of unfailing blessing to me.

I am bound to say a hearty word of thanks to Beth Bozeman, Sheila Ketteman and my wife Sylvia. Without their help my task would have been immensely more difficult.

I also appreciate the guidance and support of the editors of Evangelical Press.

Roger Ellsworth
Immanuel Baptist Church
Benton, Illinois
January 1998

Introduction

It was a Sunday evening. Two men walked slowly along the path to their village of Emmaus. Their hearts were heavy. They had hoped that Jesus of Nazareth would prove to be the Messiah the prophets had foretold, but he had died a shameful death on a Roman cross.

They were stunned. The Messiah was supposed to restore Israel to a place of supremacy among the nations. He was supposed to overthrow the Romans, not be crucified by them. Before they had absorbed all this, they became even more confused. The women who had gone early that morning to the grave claimed that Jesus was alive. What could it all mean?

Suddenly they were greeted by a stranger who noted their sadness. As they walked along with him, they poured out their story about the crucifixion of Jesus and the mysterious accounts of a resurrection.

But the stranger, instead of sympathizing with them, rebuked them. He declared that their sadness was not caused by their circumstances, but rather by their slowness to believe. Had not the prophecies of the Old Testament they professed to revere foretold the very events that had overwhelmed them — namely, the crucifixion and resurrection of Jesus? They had to learn to read those Old Testament Scriptures with new eyes. They had to understand them in terms of their crucified, risen

Messiah, who, as they were about to discover, was walking
with them. It was he of whom those Scriptures spoke.

Later that same evening, in Jerusalem, the risen Lord explicitly affirmed this same truth to another group of his disciples. According to Luke's Gospel, he 'opened their understanding, that they might comprehend the Scriptures' (Luke
24:44-45). In dealing with the sorrowing disciples on the road
to Emmaus, and with those confused disciples back in Jerusalem, the Lord Jesus rendered an inestimable service to his disciples of all ages. He showed us that we are to read the Old
Testament looking for him. He is its subject and, therefore,
the key to its understanding.

Christians readily assent to this without hesitation — until
they come to the Song of Solomon. And then that governing
principle, so readily accepted in the other books of the Old
Testament, is quickly abandoned or blissfully ignored. Why?
Because on the surface the Song of Solomon seems to be
nothing more than a celebration of romantic love between a
king and a humble maiden — appropriate enough in its way,
but what does it have to do with the Lord Jesus?

The answer might seem to be a flat, 'Nothing!' But then
we remember that the Lord Jesus Christ himself has a bride he
dearly loves (Eph. 5:25). What we have here, then, is as follows: firstly, Christ explicitly claimed to be the subject of all
the Old Testament; secondly, we have in the Song of Solomon
the celebration of love between a man and his bride; thirdly,
the Lord Jesus has a bride. We may, therefore, legitimately
take the bridegroom in the Song of Solomon as a picture of
Christ and the bride as a picture of the church.

It is my purpose in the pages that follow to discover in the
Song those descriptions of the bridegroom that have obvious
parallels in Christ, to substantiate and confirm those parallels
from other Scriptures and then seek to draw beneficial spiritual lessons from them.

This work does not claim to be an exhaustive commentary on the Song of Solomon, but rather a selection of those portions that most readily point us to Christ. Indeed, it will be necessary for us to move quite rapidly from the hints of Christ in the Song to Christ himself.

What is the purpose of all this? Let me answer that by pointing to the testimony of the two disciples with whom Jesus journeyed to Emmaus. Their hearts, they said, 'burned' within them as Christ explained to them 'in all the Scriptures the things concerning himself' (Luke 24:27,32). It is the sight of Christ that makes the Christian's heart burn. And it is the burning heart that compels us to worship and that makes our worship exhilarating business. The heart aflame also fuels our proclamation of Christ and our service to him, and steels our resolve against the opposition and ridicule of a world that knows him not.

May that burning heart be ours as we look for and find the Lord Jesus in the Song of Solomon.

Explanatory note

There are five speakers in the Song of Solomon: the Shulamite bride, the beloved groom, the daughters of Jerusalem, an unnamed relative of the bride and the brothers of the bride.

The daughters of Jerusalem are the bride's attendants. They speak with a unified voice four times (twice in 1:4; 5:9; 6:1).

The relative of the bride speaks only in 8:5, and her brothers speak only in 8:8-9. Most of the Song consists of the Shulamite's words as she speaks to her beloved and his words as he responds to her.

Section I

The excellence of Christ

1.
The fragrance of Christ

*'Because of the fragrance of your good ointments, your
name is ointment poured forth'* (S. of S. 1:3).

Smelling good is big business these days. One can scarcely
turn on the television without seeing a commercial peddling
cologne, lotion, breath mints, or deodorant. Former gener-
ations did not have our commercials, but they still had an interest in smelling good. In this verse, explaining her love for
Solomon, the Shulamite maiden admires his 'good ointments'.
She liked the fragrances she could smell when she was with
him. And when she was not with him, she enjoyed a different
fragrance, the recollection of his name. It was as if someone
had broken a jar of costly ointment and poured it out in her
presence. His name, which represented all that he was, gave
her that much pleasure.

This reference to her beloved's fragrance is only the first of
several in the Song. The Shulamite later refers to him as 'a
bundle of myrrh' (1:13) and 'a cluster of henna blooms' (1:14).
When the couple enter Jerusalem in their wedding procession,
she says:

Who is this coming out of the wilderness
Like pillars of smoke,
Perfumed with myrrh and frankincense,
With all the merchant's fragrant powders?

(3:6).

In her long description of her beloved, the Shulamite adds
these words:

> His cheeks are like a bed of spices,
> Like banks of scented herbs.
> His lips are lilies,
> Dripping liquid myrrh
>
>   (5:13).

These verses bear testimony to the strong link in the Bible
between fragrance and Christ.

The fragrance of Christ's person

Perhaps the first thing we think of in this vein are the gifts
of gold, frankincense and myrrh presented to the child Jesus
by wise men from the east (Matt. 2:1,11). They offered three
gifts, and two of these were fragrances! The gift of certain
fragrances to Jesus would not in itself be striking, were it
not for the fact that these two fragrances were used in very
definite ways.

Of frankincense (pure incense), William Hendriksen writes,
'In by far the most of the cases in which this word occurs in
the Old Testament it is mentioned in connection with the service of Jehovah.'[1] Hendriksen proceeds to note: 'In the Old
Testament the basic word *incense* occurs more than one hundred times. In the New Testament it is found in Luke 1:9-11
and Rev. 8:3,4. Whenever it occurs it has to do with the service of God... Frankincense, and also incense in general, immediately suggests God, therefore. It belongs to him, *to him
alone*. Even when it is offered to idols, God still calls it "*my*
incense" (Ezek. 16:18). It is clear, therefore, that just as *gold
and king* go together, so do also *incense and God*.'[2]

Hendriksen also provides insight into the significance of myrrh. He says, 'It was used for the purpose of perfuming a bed (Prov. 7:17) or a garment (Ps. 45:8). It was prescribed for certain young ladies, to make them more desirable (Esth. 2:12). It was also used lavishly in bridal processions (Song of Sol. 3:6). Mingled with wine it served as an anaesthetic (Mark 15:23). Finally, it was used in preparing a body for burial (John 19:39,40).'³ He summarizes by saying that it was used by mortal man 'to make his life more pleasant, his pain less dreadful, and his burial less repulsive'.⁴

Frankincense, therefore, is associated with deity and myrrh with suffering humanity. The wise men may not have realized just how appropriate their gifts were. That child was no ordinary child. He was nothing less than God in human flesh! He was God incarnate. He was fully God and fully man at one and the same time, without any contradiction between the two. He was there in Bethlehem because God, in grace that staggers the mind, had taken to himself our humanity. We are dealing here with the central claim and miracle of Christianity, tersely stated by the apostle Paul: 'God was in Christ' (2 Cor. 5:19).

This great truth evokes worship. Christians love to dwell upon it. In the incarnation of Christ, they catch the fragrant aroma of frankincense and myrrh, and gladly sing with Charles Wesley:

> Veiled in flesh, the Godhead see,
> Hail the incarnate Deity!

The fragrance of Christ's death to God

But all this raises a very important and crucial question: why? Why did the Second Person of the Trinity take to himself our humanity? Why was he made flesh? The apostle Paul gives us the answer by again linking Christ to fragrance. To the Ephesians he writes, 'Walk in love, as Christ also has loved us and given himself for us, an offering and a sacrifice to God for a sweet-smelling aroma' (Eph. 5:2).

This takes us back to the sacrificial system of the Old Testament. When Noah left the ark, he built an altar and offered clean animals and birds to the Lord, and the Lord 'smelled a soothing aroma' (Gen. 8:21). The same phrase is used to describe the Lord's response to the animal sacrifices that were offered according to the laws he gave to Moses. In Exodus 29:18 the Lord calls the burnt offering 'a sweet aroma'. When we come to the book of Leviticus, we find this phrase used again and again (1:9,13,17; 2:9,12; 3:5,16; 4:31; 6:15,21; 8:21,28; 17:6; 23:13). The book of Numbers also makes frequent use of it.

When God is said to smell the sweet aroma of sacrifices, he is pictured in terms of a man enjoying a fragrant aroma. This is, of course, an anthropomorphism — that is, it ascribes human characteristics to God. The purpose behind this picture is to tell us that there was something about those sacrifices that brought pleasure and satisfaction to God. What was there about the sacrifice of animals that would give God pleasure? Does God just enjoy the smell of burned meat? Not at all. God's pleasure in those sacrifices lay in what they represented.

When Adam and Eve fell into sin, God pronounced the sentence of death upon them. That death was far more than mere physical death (the separation of body and soul). It was also spiritual (the separation of the soul from God) and eternal (the separation of soul and body from God for ever). The only way for Adam and Eve to be redeemed from the terrible tyranny their sin had unleashed was for them to pay the penalty of death, or for someone to pay it in their stead.

It was there in the Garden of Eden, not centuries later under the law of Moses, that animal sacrifices began. God killed animals and made coats of skin for Adam and Eve (Gen. 3:21). He used these creatures as their substitutes. Their sins had, as it were, been transferred to the animals, which had thus been punished in their place by death. Those animals, of course, had no real power to atone for sin. Animals cannot pay for the sins of men. But they could and did picture the Lord Jesus Christ, who would one day come to make a perfect and effectual sacrifice for sin.

And this explains why God received pleasure from the sacrifice of those animals. It was because they pictured and anticipated the perfect offering of Christ. This representation of the death of Christ by animal sacrifices continued down the centuries until the Lord Jesus Christ finally arrived. He came for the express purpose of perfectly doing what those animal sacrifices could only faintly portray. He came to die in the place of sinners, to be the substitute for all those who believe, to suffer the penalty of death on their behalf, that they might receive eternal life. He could do this because he was fully man.

Why would the death of Christ on the cross be pleasing to God? God the Father, God the Son and God the Spirit together devised the eternal plan of redemption before time began (2 Tim. 1:9-10). Any idea that God the Son had to wring forgiveness from a reluctant Father has absolutely no basis in Scripture. It was the Father who sent the Son. It was God who caused Jesus to die there on the cross. The Son's death was pleasing to the Father because it was an act of obedience to the Father's will, and because it provided atonement for the people whom the Father loved and gave to Christ before the foundation of the world (John 17:1-2).

The fragrance of the gospel to those who believe

Scripture has yet more to say about the fragrance of Christ. His atoning death is fragrant to God, but, thank God, it is also fragrant to all those in whom the Spirit of God effectually works. The apostle Paul discusses this in his second letter to the Corinthians. There he is defending and describing his ministry as an apostle, and expresses his gratitude to God for diffusing 'the fragrance of his knowledge in every place' (2 Cor. 2:14). Then he adds this word of explanation: 'For we are to God the fragrance of Christ among those who are being saved and among those who are perishing. To the one we are the aroma of death [leading] to death, and to the other the aroma of life [leading] to life' (2 Cor. 2:15-16).

The apostle is talking about the gospel message he had been charged to preach. He asserts that this message (the message of Christ's atoning death) is fragrant to God (v. 15). There is no surprise here. If, as we saw earlier, Christ's death on the cross was fragrant to God, it is obvious that the *preaching* of that death must also be fragrant to him.

But, oh, what a needed corrective this is! It is the preaching of 'Jesus Christ and him crucified' that is fragrant to God! (1 Cor. 2:2). When we depart from this gospel to proclaim other things, we are not pleasing God. We may very well defend ourselves by talking about how 'relevant' our message is; we may be addressing those matters that are most apt to secure a large hearing, but only the gospel of God's grace in Christ, 'who was delivered for our offences, and was raised again for our justification', is fragrant to him (Rom. 4:25, AV).

That gospel is also fragrant to those in whom the Spirit of God effectually works. The message makes them aware of their situation. It tells them that they must stand before a holy God, and that he demands perfect righteousness of all those who would enter heaven. It makes clear that they have absolutely no righteousness of their own to offer God.

When the sinner realizes these things, he is driven to dark despair. But then the Spirit of God points him to the Lord Jesus. Christ has paid for the sins he has committed and has provided the righteousness that the sinner lacks. He can indeed meet God's demand for perfect righteousness by availing himself of the 'righteousness which ... is through faith in Christ' (Phil. 3:9). Casting himself totally and entirely upon the Lord Jesus, the sinner finds that there is life, eternal life, in Christ. Yes, in that gospel message he smells the fragrance of life, and what a sweet fragrance it is!

The fragrance of the gospel to those who reject it

But there is another, more solemn, dimension to this gospel message. At the same time as it emits the fragrance of life to those who receive it, it also emits the odour of death to those who reject it. Being spiritually blind, they cannot even see that they need a Saviour, and they certainly cannot see how a man dying on a Roman cross can give them eternal life. In fact they are offended at the suggestion. Because they see only death in the message of 'Christ and him crucified', they reject it, and in rejecting it they seal their own eternal death.

There is here another corrective word for preachers. The temptation today is to eliminate the odour of death from the gospel, to quietly remove all those elements that cause offence to sinners. But those elements of the gospel that offend — salvation for sinful men and women through a crucified Redeemer — are the very elements that are necessary for spiritual life. Those, therefore, who would eliminate the odour of death also eliminate the aroma of life. In other words, when we try to remove from the gospel those truths that offend people, we end up taking out the very truths that have the power to impart eternal life.

The fragrance of a coming day

Perhaps the most exhilarating of all the links between Christ and fragrance is the one we find in Psalm 45:8: 'All your garments are scented with myrrh and aloes and cassia, out of the ivory palaces, by which they have made you glad.' This psalm is about Christ and his bride, the church. There can be no doubt that this passage refers to Christ. The author of Hebrews explicitly ties it to him by quoting verses 6 and 7 (Heb. 1:8-9).

Specifically, this psalm is about the wedding of Christ and his church. Walter Chantry says of Christ in this psalm: 'He came to this earth once to betroth a bride. He has paid a handsome sum to purchase her for himself. She, of course, is the Church of the Son of God. Having the hope of his returning to accompany her into his own ivory palaces, she is preparing herself. The day of Jesus' second coming will be the wedding day of the Lamb and his bride, the Church.'[5]

On that glorious day, the church will at last fully appreciate the fragrance of her Christ.

The Christian's fragrance

We cannot leave this matter of fragrance without mentioning another aspect of fragrance in the Song of Solomon. Not only does the Shulamite speak of Solomon's fragrances; he also speaks of hers in these words:

Your plants are an orchard of pomegranates
With pleasant fruits,
Fragrant henna with spikenard,
Spikenard and saffron,
Calamus and cinnamon,
With all trees of frankincense,
Myrrh and aloes,
With all the chief spices

(4:13-14).

Just as Solomon could detect the Shulamite's many fragrances, so Christ finds much in the church that delights and pleases him. What is there about God's people that is fragrant to Christ? Firstly, they are fragrant to him because they are his Father's gift to him. Again and again in his great prayer in John 17, Jesus refers to his disciples in these terms: 'They were yours, you gave them to me, and they have kept your word' (John 17:6). Secondly, they are fragrant to Christ because they manifest the nine graces that Paul calls 'the fruit of the Spirit' — love, joy, peace, long-suffering, kindness, goodness, faithfulness, gentleness, self-control (Gal. 5:22-23). Notice that these things that Christ finds fragrant in his people are not there by nature, but are rather put there by the indwelling Spirit of Christ; they are the fruit of the Spirit, not of human nature.

Paul also refers to the sacrificial service performed on his behalf by Epaphroditus as 'a sweet-smelling aroma, an acceptable sacrifice, well pleasing to God' (Phil. 4:18). So any act of service to God or his people performed from a heart of love is fragrant to our Lord.

Finally, we find the author of Hebrews appealing to his readers to 'continually offer the sacrifice of praise to God', which he calls 'the fruit of our lips' (Heb. 13:15). He also calls the

doing of good 'sacrifices' with which God is 'well pleased'
(Heb. 13:16). It may seem at first glance as if there is nothing
in those verses about fragrance. But look at those words 'sacrifice' and 'well pleased'. They take us back to the picture of
God smelling a sweet savour in sacrifices. Just as Christ's sacrifice of himself was fragrant to God, so is the Christian's 'living sacrifice' pleasing to God (Rom. 12:1-2). The offering of
praise and worship to God and rendering of service for God
are alike fragrant to him. It is our privilege and responsibility
to see to it that we are offering up such sacrifices continually
to our Lord.

Mary of Bethany, out of a heart of love for Christ, poured
out a costly ointment on Jesus' feet and wiped them with her
hair. So lavish was this gift that the whole house was filled
with the fragrance of the oil (John 12:3). As we think about
the fragrant ointments we have in Christ, it should be our desire to lavish the precious ointment of our own lives upon him,
in worship and service, so that the fragrance will be known to
all around us. 'Let your light so shine before men', said the
Lord Jesus, 'that they may see your good works and glorify
your Father in heaven' (Matt. 5:16).

2.
Christ proclaiming his excellence

'I am the rose of Sharon, and the lily of the valleys'
(S.of S. 2:1).

In this verse, the Shulamite's beloved, King Solomon, speaks of himself as 'the rose of Sharon and the lily of the valleys'. This was his way of proclaiming his own excellence. There can be little doubt about the way Scripture relates these particular flowers to excellence and perfection. The rose of Sharon represents beauty and excellence in a well-known passage from Isaiah:

> The wilderness and the wasteland shall be glad for them,
> And the desert shall rejoice and blossom as the rose;
> It shall blossom abundantly and rejoice,
> Even with joy and singing.
> The glory of Lebanon shall be given to it,
> The excellence of Carmel and Sharon.
> They shall see the glory of the LORD,
> The excellency of our God
>
> (Isa. 35:1-2).

There is little agreement on which modern flower corresponds to the rose of Scripture. It was certainly not what we call a rose today. Most commentators seem to favour the narcissus which grew in dazzling abundance on the plain of Sharon, a fertile tract on the Mediterranean coast. Others think the flower referred to is the crimson anemone. Whatever the precise identity of the flower, however, it is beyond dispute that it was associated with beauty and excellence.

The lily is also a symbol of elegance and beauty. A stately plant of six leaves and six petals, it grew to four feet or more in height and was often used for decorative purposes (1 Kings 7:19,22,26). The Lord Jesus himself gave this testimony to the excellence of the lily: 'Even Solomon in all his glory was not arrayed like one of these' (Matt. 6:28-29).

The main controversy that surrounds this passage does not, however, have to do with the identity of the flowers, but rather with that of the speaker. There is considerable doubt among commentators about whether these words belong to the beloved. The argument is that Solomon could not possibly have referred to himself as the rose and the lily because that would have been far too presumptuous and arrogant of him. They suggest, therefore, that this is the bride's way of saying she was as common as these flowers.

I have two answers to that objection. Firstly, the glory and magnificence of Solomon's kingdom were such that it was indeed possible for him to speak in this way without being boastful and proud. Secondly, in this song Solomon represents the Lord Jesus Christ. In other words, this song was not given to the church merely as a glimpse into one of Solomon's romantic relationships, but to enable her to see her Lord. In dealing with this song, therefore, we must always move quickly from the Shulamite's beloved, Solomon, to the church's beloved, Christ. The fact is that, down the ages, these words have been seen by many Christians, if not by most, as a perfect description of their Lord. Some well-known hymns illustrate this point. One says:

Jesus, Rock of Ages, let me hide in thee,
Jesus, Rose of Sharon, sweet thou art to me,

Lily of the Valley, Bright and Morning Star,
Fairest of ten thousand to my soul.

(Anon.)

Another declares:

He's the Lily of the Valley
The bright and morning Star,
He's the fairest of ten thousand to my soul.

(Charles W. Frey)

Whatever we say about the appropriateness of Solomon's speaking these words about himself, this much is beyond dispute: it is entirely appropriate for the Lord Jesus Christ to proclaim his own excellence. His outspoken testimony concerning himself was that 'A greater than Solomon is here' (Matt. 12:42).

Not only do we deem it appropriate for our Lord to proclaim his own excellence, but there are many passages in Scripture where he actually did so. Nowhere do we find such proclamations more frequent and forceful than in the writings of the apostle John. In his Gospel alone we find seven 'I am' sayings from the Saviour. One of these, 'I am the good shepherd,' will receive our attention in chapter seven. Here we briefly consider the remaining 'I am' sayings from John's Gospel and two from the book of Revelation.

'I am the bread of life' (John 6:35,48,51)

It was the day after Jesus had miraculously fed a multitude in the wilderness. 'Who is this Jesus?' was the pulsating question in the minds of the people. If only he would perform an additional sign! Feeding a multitude was quite a feat, but it

was not, as far as they were concerned, on a par with what
Moses had done for their fathers centuries before. Moses fed
them in the wilderness with bread from heaven. He did not
even start out with five loaves and two fishes as Jesus had
done. And he did it, not just once, but for forty years. Nor did
he do it for a mere five thousand, but for several hundred
thousand!

Jesus knew what they were thinking. He also knew how to
respond to them. First, he pointed out that it was not Moses at
all who fed their fathers in the wilderness, but rather God (John
6:32).

Secondly, he pointed out that the manna their fathers ate in
the wilderness was just physical food. It could feed the body,
but not the soul. The same God that had sent their fathers
manna had now done something far greater. He had sent them
true bread, spiritual bread, that would give them spiritual life.
It would so feed their hungry souls that they would never hunger again. Jesus was that bread. To 'eat' it, they had to believe
in him as the one sent from God and the only one who could
give them eternal life (John 6:40,47). How excellent is Christ!

'I am the light of the world' (John 8:12)

The Bible constantly uses darkness as an emblem for man in
his natural state of sin and separation from God. Sinners are
said to have their hearts darkened (Rom. 1:21), as well as
their understanding (Eph. 4:18). Their minds are darkened
because Satan, who is the prince of darkness and who rules
over the kingdom of darkness (Eph. 6:12), has blinded their
minds (2 Cor. 4:4). Because men are so blinded they love darkness rather than light (John 3:19) and do 'the unfruitful works
of darkness' (Eph. 5:11).

The Christian was also, of course, in this state at one time. The apostle Paul says we were 'by nature children of wrath, just as the others' — that is, just like everyone else (Eph. 2:3). But that is no longer our condition. A marvellous transformation has taken place. We have been called out of darkness into light (1 Peter 2:9) and are now 'sons of light and sons of the day' (1 Thess. 5:5). Paul says, 'We are not of the night nor of darkness' (1 Thess. 5:5).

How did this glorious change come about? Through the Lord Jesus Christ. He is the only light that can dispel the darkness of sin, and he has graciously shone in our hearts: 'God ... has shone in our hearts to give the light of the knowledge of the glory of God in the face of Jesus Christ' (2 Cor. 4:6). Oh, the excellence of Christ!

'I am the door' (John 10:9)

Christ again proclaimed his excellence when he was contrasting himself with the religious leaders of the day. These leaders had just cast out of the synagogue the blind man whom Jesus had healed (John 9:1-34). This callous act marked them out as false shepherds who had no real concern for the people and no understanding of how to lead them to spiritual life.

With the metaphor of the door the Lord Jesus showed that he, and he alone, is the model for all shepherds. In other words, he is the standard by which we must judge whether a man is a true minister or not. Entering by the door into the sheepfold, the true minister is recognized by the sheep and is able to lead them. In other words, the true minister is Christ-centred. He has himself entered the sheepfold by the door — that is, through faith in Jesus as Lord and Saviour — and now preaches Christ to others. For their part, the people of God instinctively know the Christ-centred man is of God, for he bids them follow Christ, the Chief Shepherd (1 Peter 5:4).

The false minister, on the other hand, does not use the door. Nor does he preach the coming and dying of Christ as the only means of salvation, or seek to glorify and exalt Christ. By various means, he tries to get the sheep to follow himself rather than Christ. The final result of this approach is death. That is why Jesus says the thief kills and destroys (John 10:10). Mark it well. Any ministry that does not preach Christ does not save souls, but rather kills them.

'I am the resurrection and the life' (John 11:25)

Here Jesus proclaims his excellence in terms of his mastery over death. Mary and Martha were crushed. Their brother Lazarus had died. They had hoped that Jesus would come and heal him of his illness, but their Master had delayed, and now Lazarus had been in his tomb for four days.

When the Lord arrived, Martha met him with these words of reproach: 'Lord, if you had been here, my brother would not have died' (John 11:21). She knew Lazarus would rise again at the end of time (John 11:24), but she did not fully appreciate that she was speaking, even at that moment, to the one who is 'the resurrection and the life'.

Jesus' affirmation not only had immediate relevance for Martha and her situation but also for all believers. Because Jesus is the resurrection and life, we have the confidence that our bodies will some day be raised from the grave. But, thank God, this is not all. Because Jesus is the resurrection and the life, believers also know that there is a sense in which they will never die. Jesus has already exercised his resurrection power in them by raising them from spiritual death to spiritual life (Eph. 2:4-6). While they still die physically, they can never die spiritually or eternally. How excellent is Christ!

'I am the way, the truth, and the life' (John 14:6)

It was the night before our Lord was crucified. Jesus was in the upper room with his disciples. He had just made a glorious statement about heaven, calling it a place of 'many mansions' and 'my Father's house'. He had assured the disciples that he would return and take them there (John 14:1-3). Jesus wrapped it all up by saying, 'And where I go you know, and the way you know' (John 14:4).

That statement sparked a puzzled response from Thomas: 'Lord, we do not know where you are going, and how can we know the way?' (John 14:5). It was that question that prompted Jesus to say, 'I am the way, the truth, and the life.'

A 'way' connects two points. It gives us the means to move from one of those points to the other. The question of all questions, as far as the Bible is concerned, is how can guilty sinners move from the point of their sin and their guilt to the point of acceptance with a holy God?

The answer is Jesus Christ. He is the way to heaven's glory. He is the one who can lead us from sin to salvation, from condemnation before God to peace with God, from hell to heaven. How is Jesus the way? What is there about him that makes him the way? The other two words he uses in his 'I am' saying give us the answer — he is the truth and the life. Jesus is the way because he shows us the truth about our condition and about God's gracious provision for our deliverance. He also implements that deliverance, granting us the gift of spiritual life.

Do you see the significance of this? The Bible says our problem is that by nature we are blind to our sinful condition and our standing before God. We do not even see that we need a way out of our sins and into heaven, much less that Jesus is that way. The Bible also tells us that we are dead in our sins (Eph. 2:1). We have absolutely no power in and of ourselves to do anything about our condition.

Even if we could somehow see that Jesus is the way to heaven — a considerable feat for dead people — we have absolutely no power to take that path. We do not have it in ourselves to repent of our sins and to trust Christ as Saviour. So Jesus becomes the way to heaven for sinners by doing two things: he opens our eyes to see that we need a way to God, and he gives us life so that we can walk in that way. How excellent is Christ!

'I am the vine' (John 15:1,5)

It is the grand purpose of God for our lives that we bear fruit for him. He wants us to reflect his image, to obey his commands and to live for his glory. Sin has kept us from bearing the fruit that God demands and to which he is entitled, and God would have been completely justified in uprooting and discarding us.

But God refused to be thwarted by sin and planted a vine through which he could secure fruit from us. That vine is his Son, the Lord Jesus Christ. He is the only way that we are able to bring forth fruit unto God. To bear the fruit that God demands of us, then, we must be vitally connected to Christ, the true vine. That connection, or 'abiding', is brought about through faith. How excellent is Christ!

'I am the Alpha and the Omega' (Rev. 1:8,17; 22:13)

We find further 'I am' sayings in the book of Revelation. Alpha is the first letter of the Greek alphabet, and omega the last. Jesus claims, therefore, to be the beginning and the end. It is a powerful and graphic assertion of his complete sovereignty. Nothing falls outside of it. And it is also a powerful assertion of his fulness and constancy. He is from beginning to end the eternal God.

Geoffrey Wilson cites the words of Richard of St Victor on Christ's claim to be the First and the Last: 'First, because before me a God was not formed; last, because after me there shall not be another. First, because all things are from me; last, because all things are to me; from me the beginning, to me the end. First, because I am the cause of origin; last, because I am the judge and the end.'[1]

'I am alive for evermore' (Rev. 1:18)

Because Jesus Christ is fully God, he has 'life in himself' (John 5:26). Life is a divine attribute, part and parcel of God. But, wonder of wonders, the Lord Jesus, who possessed life and is the source of life, actually died. Added to that is a second wonder: he arose from the dead, never to die again.

The implications of Christ's excellence

Even with all these statements, we have barely scratched the surface of Christ's proclamation of his own excellence. In addition to these 'I am' sayings, we find Christ proclaiming his excellence in other terms. He claims to be the one sent from heaven (John 3:13), to have the power to give living water (John 4:14), and to do the will of God perfectly (John 5:19,30). We could go on and on. But do we understand the significance of all this?

The glorious excellence of Christ is an awesome thing because, in the first place, it takes a considerable variety of figures and expressions to give us even a faint glimpse of it. It is also awesome that Christ would condescend to proclaim his own excellence. It is, after all, an act of condescension. If Christ had not proclaimed his own excellence to us, we would know little about it. No one else could do it. No one has entered heaven and made a study of these things. But, thank God, Christ has come down from heaven to declare them.

The excellence of Christ also places upon us the responsibility not only to admire it, but also to appropriate it. Let me explain this by returning to the rose of Sharon and the lily of the valleys. Sharon was the name of a plain that runs for fifty miles, from modern Tel-Aviv to just south of Mt Carmel. This plain was covered with flowers that could easily be picked by anyone who happened to be walking along. Similarly, the lilies that grew in the valleys were also easy to find and pick. Had these flowers been found only on the mountain-tops, it would have been difficult to find and pick them. But walking through a valley is easy. There are many beautiful things in this life that we cannot possess or enjoy, but anyone can pick a rose or lily growing by the way.

So it is with Christ. His excellence can be enjoyed by all who believe, because he has made himself accessible to us. He has stepped down from the mountain of his glory to the lowlands of our humiliation, the human condition in which we sinful people live. And there he has caused his excellence to bloom before our eyes. Now, through the Scriptures, he invites us personally to appropriate and enjoy his excellence. Possess the flowers of Christ's excellence, smell their fragrance, admire their beauty. This is what Scripture urges us to do.

3.
The church proclaims him flawless

'"What is your beloved more than another beloved, O fairest among women?" ... "My beloved is white and ruddy, chief among ten thousand... He is altogether lovely"'
(S. of S. 5:9–10,16).

With these verses we come to the fullest picture of Christ in the whole Song. Here the bride gives a detailed description of the bridegroom, a description which may be taken as the church speaking of her Lord. The question that prompted the description was posed by the daughters of Jerusalem: 'What is your beloved more than another beloved?'

The word 'beloved' indicates a superior or surpassing love. It is applied to that object or person upon which we bestow our highest love and fondest affection. The daughters of Jerusalem did not ask who was the object of the bride's greatest affection. They knew that. Their question was rather *why* she set her affection upon her beloved. What was there about him that made him so special, that set him above all the other persons and objects on which she could have bestowed her most fervent love?

The bride was not at a loss for an answer. She was eager to respond. She made no apology for making her love for her beloved so obvious. As proud grandparents are always ready to whip out the pictures of their grandchildren, so she was ready to talk about her beloved. I can hear her now: 'Do you want to hear about my beloved? Let me tell you.' And off she goes on the long description we find in verses 10-16.

Let's face it. The question of the daughters of Jerusalem
puts squarely before us a thrilling possibility — it is possible
for God's children to so love Christ, and as a result to live in
such a way, that they arrest attention and arouse interest. The
reverse side of the coin is sombre. It is also possible for God's
children to live in such a way that they never stimulate in others
any thought about their faith or provoke any consideration of
it. The apostle Peter tells his readers to 'Always be ready to
give a defence to everyone who asks you a reason for the
hope that is in you' (1 Peter 3:15). He expected them to live in
such an arresting manner that they would frequently have to
explain why Christ meant so much to them.

This description of the beloved consists of two major parts.
It opens and closes with phrases that may be considered general in nature. I am thinking here of the expressions 'white and
ruddy' (v. 10), 'chief among ten thousand' (v. 10) and 'altogether lovely' (v. 16).

The bride could not be content, however, to only give a
general answer to the question of her friends. One characteristic of people in love is that they relish details. So in verses
11-16, the Shulamite proceeds to give a very detailed description of the various parts of her beloved's body. Both the general phrases and the particular details must, of course, be related to the Lord Jesus Christ. As the bride proclaimed the
excellence of her beloved, so the church of Christ eagerly and
readily proclaims the excellence of her Saviour.

The affirmations of his flawlessness

One thing the church loves to focus on in her proclamation of
Christ is his flawlessness. Each of the bride's general statements about her beloved may be connected with the flawlessness of Christ. The first and last of these phrases may be regarded as the bride affirming the same thing in different ways.

The middle phrase, 'chief among ten thousand,' may be regarded as an implication or result of his flawlessness.

The Shulamite's first phrase is 'white and ruddy'. This indicates that her beloved was perfect in beauty, that he had no flaw or deficiency in his complexion. George Burrowes says, 'When it is said, the beloved is white and ruddy, the meaning is, that his complexion is the perfection of beauty and health. David was "ruddy and withal of beautiful countenance, and goodly to look to." '[1] The phrase 'altogether lovely' means, in the words of Stuart Olyott, that he was 'without defect, fault or blemish'. Olyott adds, 'There is nothing imperfect or spoiled about him. Everything about him is desirable.'[2]

Such exalted terms were quite extravagant when applied to Solomon, but they are not the least bit overdone when applied to Christ. Scripture boldly asserts that Christ was indeed perfect in beauty, without flaw, in every aspect of his person, life and ministry. Of him, John Flavel writes, 'His excellencies are pure and unmixed; he is a sea of sweetness without one drop of gall.'[3]

No flaw in Christ's person

There is no flaw to be found in his person. He is fully God and fully man. Some commentators take the phrase 'white and ruddy' to be a happy way of picturing the two natures of Christ. They take 'white' to represent his deity and 'ruddy' (red) to represent his human nature (flesh and blood). This may be reading too much into the text, but this much is beyond dispute — there is no flaw to be found in the person of Christ.

There is no deficiency or defect in his deity, for 'In him dwells all the fulness of the Godhead bodily' (Col. 2:9). His person is by its very nature incapable of imperfection.

But what about the humanity of Christ? Surely he could not take our humanity without inheriting our sin? The Bible most emphatically assures us that he did. Without losing any of his deity, the Second Person of the Trinity assumed our humanity. In doing so he was conceived by the Holy Spirit and born of a virgin. Having no human father, he received a humanity that was flawless, devoid of original sin. But he still had to live out that humanity in a sinful world. Does that mean that, as a consequence, he was soiled or tainted by sin? No, the testimony of Scripture is that he remained 'without sin'; no flaw could be found in his life.

All other human beings, no matter how saintly their lives, or how sterling their accomplishments, have committed sins along the way, for 'If we say that we have no sin, we deceive ourselves' (1 John 1:8). But the uniform testimony of Holy Scripture is that the Lord Jesus was absolutely without spot or blemish. The prophet Isaiah foretold this, saying that Christ would do no violence, nor would any deceit be found in his mouth (Isa. 53:9).

Jesus' disciples lived in the closest possible association with him for more than three years. The apostle John makes it clear that they were not just with him during those years, but that they closely studied and scrutinized him. In his Gospel, John says he and the other disciples 'beheld' Jesus (John 1:14). In other words, they intently and steadily gazed at him. Theirs was not just a quick, cursory glance. By using this word, John was putting on record that his conclusions about Jesus were not casually or lightly formed, but were the result of careful and prolonged observation.

In his first epistle, John writes more about his experience with Jesus. He says he and the other disciples not only heard and saw Jesus, but they 'looked upon' him and 'handled' him (1 John 1:1). These are the phrases of close and familiar association. They indicate that John and the other disciples had, as it were, placed Jesus under the closest possible scrutiny and had come away with the abiding conviction that he was nothing less than 'the only begotten of the Father, full of grace and truth' (John 1:14). Thus John leaves us in no doubt at all about the perfection of Jesus the man: 'In him there is no sin' (1 John 3:5).

The truly remarkable thing about the witness of these men to the sinlessness of Jesus is that they were not disposed by their training to accept such a thing. They were steeped in the teachings of the Old Testament and were, therefore, firm believers in the universality of sin (Ps. 14:2-3; 53:1-3; Eccles. 7:20; Isa. 53:6). But when they looked at Jesus, they knew they were looking at a glorious exception.

It was not only the disciples who were convinced on the subject. When Jesus was taken to trial before Pontius Pilate, the pronouncement made was this: 'I find no fault in him at all' (John 18:38). Pilate may have been talking about legal fault, but he was also unwittingly saying the very same thing that all the Scriptures tell us about Christ — namely, that he was completely without sin.

Why was it so important that Christ was without sin? The apostle answers our question when he calls Jesus 'a lamb without blemish and without spot' (1 Peter 1:19). Only a perfect human being could act as the substitute and sacrifice for our sins. If he were not without sin, he could die only for his own sins, not for ours. It is because he was flawless that he could offer himself for our sins, 'the just for the unjust', and have that sacrifice accepted by the Father.

No flaw in Christ's teaching

There is no flaw to be found in his teaching. The common people heard him gladly. His enemies tried to find fault with his teachings, but each time they challenged him they were sent away bewildered and confused. This is not surprising. Centuries before the Lord Jesus Christ came to this earth, Moses said to the people of Israel, 'The Lord your God will raise up for you a Prophet like me from your midst, from your brethren. Him you shall hear' (Deut. 18:15).

The duty of the prophet was to speak to men on behalf of God. Jesus was the prophet *par excellence*. In John's Gospel we find him saying, 'As my Father taught me, I speak these things' (John 8:28). Later our Lord spoke these words: 'I have not spoken on my own authority; but the Father who sent me gave me a command, what I should say and what I should speak. And I know that his command is everlasting life. Therefore, whatever I speak, just as the Father has told me, so I speak' (John 12:49-50). Christ's words are the words of God and we must heed them. As the writer to the Hebrews puts it, 'See that you do not refuse him who speaks. For if they did not escape who refused him who spoke on earth [Moses], much more shall we not escape if we turn away from him who speaks from heaven [God speaking in Christ]' (Heb. 12:25).

No flaw in Christ's work

As there is no flaw in Jesus' teaching, so there is no flaw to be found in the work he came to perform. He came to this world to perform a specific task, the task of redemption. In accordance with the plan upon which he and the Father agreed before the world began, Jesus came to this earth to provide eternal salvation for all those who believe.

We make plans, but they are only rarely carried out without difficulties arising. They always have to be adjusted and changed, and sometimes completely abandoned. Human plans are subject to fits and starts, to frustrations and hitches. But there were no hitches when Christ came to carry out heaven's plan. No one can point to a single episode in Jesus' life and say, 'Ah, he had to abandon his plan!' No one can even find an instance in which he had to modify his plans.

Jesus came to carry out meticulously that heavenly design. We find him saying, 'My food is to do the will of him who sent me, and to finish his work' (John 4:34). He further says, 'I do not seek my own will but the will of the Father who sent me' (John 5:30). Again he declares, 'For I have come down from heaven, not to do my own will, but the will of him who sent me' (John 6:38). While he was engaged in carrying out the Father's plan, Jesus was able to say, 'I always do those things that please him' (John 8:29).

Some look at the cross and think they have found a flaw in the plan. They think Christ came to set up an earthly kingdom but was thrown off course. Rejected by his own, he found it impossible to go through with his original intention and chose to suffer martyrdom on the cross as a backup plan. Those who hold this view go so far as to suggest that the age in which we are now, the so-called 'church age', is a 'parenthesis' in human history, forced upon God by circumstances beyond his control.

Over against this argument stands the simple, sublime statement of Scripture that Jesus Christ was 'the Lamb slain from the foundation of the world' (Rev. 13:8). The cross was no afterthought with God, and it did not take Jesus by surprise. He went there deliberately, 'by the determined counsel [or "carefully planned intention"] and foreknowledge of God' (Acts 2:23), to redeem his people by taking their place. His cry, 'It is finished!' (John 19:30), proves the cross was the plan of God all along.

And there is no flaw to be found in the salvation that he provided on that cross. It fully paid the price. It delivered his elect from eternal wrath. It sealed hell's door. It opened heaven's door. It purchased the gift of the Holy Spirit to call the sinner to Christ, and to seal him until that grand, sparkling day when redemption will finally be complete and, to quote Charles Wesley, we shall all be 'lost in wonder, love, and praise'.

Sceptics have ridiculed the notion of eternal salvation being provided through a bloody death on a Roman cross, but
Christians have experienced that salvation and eagerly proclaim with Paul that there is no flaw in that plan, but that what
is foolishness to men is indeed the very power and wisdom of
God (1 Cor. 1:18–25).

The implications of Christ's flawlessness

Is Christ indeed 'white and ruddy'? Is he indeed 'altogether
lovely'? Then the Christian is quickly driven to pick up the
third of the Shulamite's general phrases, and declare that Christ
is 'chief among ten thousand' (5:10).

By using this expression, the Shulamite was asserting that
her beloved was without peer or rival. The phrase is borrowed
from the battlefield and refers to a standard-bearer in an army.
The standard was the rallying-point, that point to which all
eyes turned. It towered above the soldiers' heads and was the
centre of attraction.

The bride was suggesting, therefore, that her beloved stood
out from among men. All others belong to the masses of mankind, but even as a man he stands head and shoulders above
them all. She was saying, as John Gill suggests, 'There may be
ten thousand persons that carry a flag, but none to be compared with him, for comeliness, strength, and courage.'[4] He
towers above men even as the standard-bearer stood out above
the soldiers of the army.

In the words of George Burrowes, 'The believer feels most
truly, that wherever he goes, under all circumstances, Jesus is,
like the banner in an armed host, the centre of attraction to
which his eyes are always anxiously turned, the rallying point
of his soul, full high advanced above all others; the splendour
of his divinity burning with a brilliancy of glory richer than a

meteor streaming to the wind, brighter than the cloud that rested on the mount of transfiguration.'[5]

The flawlessness of Jesus means no one else is in the same class with him. He is not one flawless person among many. He alone is the flawless one. Bring your greatest political leaders and statesmen, your most eminent philosophers and religious leaders, your finest educators and scientists. Bring whom you wish and compare them to Jesus of Nazareth. Invariably you will find their greatness tainted with sin and self, but the Lord Jesus, after years of scrutiny and study, remains untainted. His lustre is untarnished, his beauty undiminished.

4.
The church proclaims his beauty

'His head is like the finest gold... His countenance is like Lebanon...' (S. of S. 5:11–15).

We saw above that the Shulamite's answer to the question posed by the daughters of Jerusalem consists of two major parts: general and particular. In the previous chapter we examined the general phrases found at the beginning and the end of her description of the beloved. Now we come to the details. There are a great many particulars here, and all of them reflect the church's praise of her Lord. But there is something of a natural division among these details. With some the Shulamite praises the beauty of her beloved, and with others his strength.

We shall attempt, therefore, to gather all her descriptions under these two headings, beauty and strength, and try to hear in them the voice of the church praising the beauty and strength of Christ. In doing so, however, we shall omit the mouth and lips, since these will be considered in later chapters.

The golden head of Christ

The first of the Shulamite's detailed descriptions deals with the head of her beloved, a head that was 'like the finest gold' (5:11). It is obvious that this young woman enjoyed looking at her beloved. As she gazed upon him, she seems to have imagined a sculptor standing back to admire a bust he had just

completed. The sculptor, she thought, had a special reason to
be proud of his work. Busts are usually sculpted out of stone
or bronze, materials that are admirable enough, but this bust
had been sculpted from the finest gold.

With this figure, the young woman is telling us how admirable, precious and glorious is the beloved in her eyes, and
how much she delights in him. How can the Christian apply
this to his Beloved, the Lord Jesus? Generally, we may say we
receive exquisite delight from looking upon Christ as he is
revealed to us in Holy Scripture. But we can go beyond this
generality to identify particular traits or features of Christ.

Think about the two things that are laid before us in this
phrase, 'His head is like the finest gold.' What does the head
represent? In his letter to the Ephesians, the apostle Paul says
Christ has been exalted above all 'principality and power and
might and dominion', has had all things put 'under his feet',
and has been made 'head over all things' (Eph. 1:21-23). A
little later in the same letter, he tells us that the Lord Jesus is
'head of the church' (Eph. 5:23). The head, then, represents
rule or dominion.

Think about gold for a moment. What does it represent?
Generally, we may say it represents excellence and glory. More
specifically, we can say it represents beauty and durability. Now
apply these things to the Lord Jesus Christ and here is what
we come up with: Jesus Christ has dominion, or rule, and that
dominion is excellent, glorious, beautiful and eternal.

The mystery of Christ's rule

Does it seem strange to hear of Christ ruling today? As far as
many are concerned, the idea is patently absurd. They look at
the world and see evil all around. They look at the church and
they see apathy and feebleness. They look at the Scriptures
and they see those verses that speak of Satan as the ruler of

this world (2 Cor. 4:4; Eph. 6:11-12). The conclusion seems indisputable: Christ may rule some day, but he is not ruling now! Thank God, the reality is not as depressing as these thoughts seem to imply.

In addition to those Scriptures which assert that Satan rules this fallen world are many that affirm the over-arching sovereignty of God and of his Christ. David asserts this when he prays regarding his enemies: 'Let them know that God rules in Jacob to the ends of the earth' (Ps. 59:13). An unnamed psalmist also declares God's rule: 'He rules by his power for ever... ' (Ps. 66:7). Even the pagan king Nebuchadnezzar was forced to admit the rule of God. 'The Most High rules in the kingdom of men', he declares and goes on to say,

> His dominion is an everlasting dominion...
> He does according to his will in the army of heaven
> And among the inhabitants of the earth.
> No one can restrain his hand
> Or say to him, "What have you done?" '
>
> (Dan. 4:17,34-35).

The New Testament is equally clear. God is the one 'who works all things according to the counsel of his will' (Eph. 1:11).

How are we to reconcile such verses with those that seem to indicate Satan is ruling? In this way: Satan's rule, while oppressively real, is secondary and limited. In other words, he rules the wickedness of this world, not because he has absolute power or authority, but rather because God permits him to do so. We must be clear at this point. Christians are not dualists. We do not believe there are two beings of equal power locked in mortal combat to see who will win. There is only one supreme power, God, and his victory over Satan is not in doubt.

But why does God allow Satan to rule in this temporary and limited way? This is the question that has baffled and bewildered believers and unbelievers alike down the running centuries. The general answer is, of course, that it pleases God to do so. More specifically, we can say that by allowing Satan this local and temporary rule, God shows the true nature of evil and reveals his grace and glory in defeating it. So things are not as they appear. Evil may look terribly strong, and even invincible, but the God of heaven is stronger than the god of this world and will triumph over him. Indeed, he has already triumphed in that he has raised Christ from the dead and seated him at his right hand, 'waiting till his enemies are made his footstool' (Heb. 10:13).

The Christian is one who is able to see through the raging sea of evil to a deeper reality, namely that the golden sceptre of Christ the king rules over all (Heb. 1:8-9). Not only does the Christian see the ruling hand of God, but he admires it and delights in it, as the Shulamite admired the beloved's head of gold.

The wisdom of Christ's rule

As the believer contemplates Christ's rule, he sees an amazing and incredible beauty. Where is the beauty of God's rule in a world such as this? It is right here: God takes the evil of this world and uses it and overrules it for his purposes and his glory.

Take the case of Joseph in the Old Testament. He was hated by his brothers and sold into slavery in Egypt. He was falsely accused by his master's wife and tossed into prison. He was forgotten and left to languish by those he helped. A cursory glance at this story might cause one to say, 'There is no beauty, no justice, here but only evil.' But look again. It was shameful that Joseph was sold into slavery. It was evil that he was framed and imprisoned. But God used all that evil to ensure that Joseph was in the right place, Egypt, at the right time. When Pharaoh needed an interpreter for his dream, Joseph was immediately available in Pharaoh's gaol! With perfect timing, God raised him from the depths of that dark dungeon to a position of authority that was second only to Pharaoh's.

Joseph certainly saw beauty in all this because we find him saying to his brothers, 'But as for you, you meant evil against me; but God meant it for good, in order to bring it about as it is this day, to save many people alive' (Gen. 50:20). Look at your own circumstances and you might see no beauty there either. But faith sees beyond what is visible and, with the apostle Paul, declares, 'We know that all things work together for good to those who love God, to those who are the called according to his purpose' (Rom. 8:28).

The durability of Christ's rule

The Christian also sees the durability of Christ's rule. Throughout human history there have been many times when evil seemed out of God's control, when it was unleashed and threatened to overthrow the rule of Christ. Adam and Eve were involved in the cataclysm of the Fall, yet God gave them the promise of a coming Saviour. They had two sons, and the promise seemed sure, but then one son killed the other. The promise was suddenly hanging by a thread, but God gave Adam and Eve another son and the promise was again secure.

Noah's generation was so wicked that it seemed that God's promises would finally be thwarted. But God spared Noah and his family and through them gave humanity a new start. God chose Abraham to be the one from whom the Messiah would spring. But Abraham had no son, and as he and his wife grew old, it once again looked as if God's purpose had come to a screeching halt. Yet, miraculously, God gave them a son in their old age.

On and on we could go. The Messiah was to come from David's line, but the descendants of David dwindled to a solitary child and even his life was in imminent peril from the wicked Queen Athaliah. But God brought that young man to the throne. Remember how God preserved the nation of Israel through the captivity and in the wilderness. When the Lord Jesus was finally born, Herod murdered all the young children in an attempt to kill him. All these were instances in which it seemed that the sovereignty of God was lost, but each time God's purposes prevailed.

Read these accounts and let your faith grow strong and robust. The evil of our day may seem unconquerable. The rule of Christ may appear at times to flag and fail. But that rule is like enduring gold. It is going to last! 'For his dominion is an everlasting dominion, and his kingdom is from generation to generation' (Dan. 4:34). As Gabriel pronounced to Mary, 'He will reign over the house of Jacob for ever, and of his kingdom there will be no end' (Luke 1:33).

The eyes of Christ

When she comes to the eyes of her beloved, the young woman employs three figures in quick succession. She first mentions doves bathing in the river. Then she speaks of them as 'washed with milk'. Finally, she describes his eyes as being 'fitly set', as a jeweller skilfully and carefully sets a gem in a ring (5:12). It seems as if the eyes of the beloved made such an impression upon her that she was not content to compare them to just one thing.

What was she saying about the eyes with these three figures? By likening them to doves, the bride indicates the gentleness and sympathy of those eyes. By depicting them as doves bathing in the water, she indicates their clear, sparkling quality. It was that quality that caused her to go further and say his eyes were such that it was as if they had been washed in milk. When she compared her beloved's eyes to the skilful work of a jeweller, the bride was affirming their perfect beauty. They were perfectly set in their sockets, not protruding and not sunken.

When we apply these figures to Christ, we must say he also has 'eyes like doves, washed in milk, and fitly set'. We may say this because we find in him the perfect expression of tenderness and gentleness, the perfect expression of sparkling discernment, alertness and intelligence and perfect beauty.

His tenderness

What compassion and tenderness we find in the eyes of Jesus! A rich young man came running to him to ask the way of eternal life and 'Jesus, looking at him, loved him...' (Mark 10:21). That same compassion was there when Jesus looked upon a vast multitude and saw that they were 'like sheep not having a shepherd'. Mark tells us that the sight of that multitude caused our Lord's heart to be 'moved with compassion' (Mark 6:34). Those of us who know the Lord might say we are saved because those eyes saw us in our sin and guilt but looked upon us in compassion. Since that time he has watched over us with tender care. He says to each of his people today, in the words in Isaiah's prophecy:

> Can a woman forget her nursing child,
> And not have compassion on the son of her womb?
> Surely they may forget,
> Yet I will not forget you.
>
> (Isa. 49:15-16).

The tenderness of the eyes of Christ is a precious thought, but we must not allow it to obscure another truth. The apostle John saw those eyes burning 'like a flame of fire' (Rev. 1:14).

Those same eyes that gleam with compassion for God's people will also burn with fierce wrath and condemnation towards those who trample the gospel of Christ under their feet.

His discernment

Those same eyes that behold us with tenderness and compassion are also keen and discerning. Nothing is hidden from them. The psalmist says, 'The eyes of the Lord are on the righteous, and his ears are open to their cry' (Ps. 34:15). And Job says of the Lord, 'He does not withdraw his eyes from the righteous' (Job. 36:7). The prophet Hanani adds these powerful words: 'For the eyes of the Lord run to and fro throughout the whole earth, to show himself strong on behalf of those whose heart is loyal to him' (2 Chron. 16:9).

His beauty

This aspect of Christ's person is, of course, celebrated throughout the Scriptures, not least in the Song of Solomon. The jeweller's art reminds us of the following truths:

the perfection of his divine nature, for 'In him dwells all the fulness of the Godhead bodily' (Col. 2:9);

the perfect balance of divine and human attributes, for he is both Son of God and Son of Man;

the perfection of his saving work, for 'He has perfected for ever those who are being sanctified' (Heb. 10:14);

and the perfection of his eternal purpose, for he will present the church to himself as 'a glorious church, not having spot or wrinkle or any such thing, but ... holy and without blemish' (Eph. 5:27).

The consolation of these truths

What consolations we have in the eyes of Christ! Because they are constantly upon us, nothing escapes their notice. Because they are tender and caring, they observe us for our good.

What, then, is that burden you carry today? Rest assured the Lord knows about it. What is that pain and anguish you feel? The Lord knows and cares about it. What is that fear that gnaws at you? The Lord sees it as well. What is that disappointment that pierces your heart? The Lord sees and cares. No matter how heavy our burdens, no matter how fearsome our trials, we have a kind, sympathizing Christ who sees with discerning eye and perfect designs. He watches us in order to discern, and he discerns in order that he may strengthen and help us.

When the young woman thought about the tenderness and compassion of her beloved's eyes, and the keen discernment of those eyes, she could not help but say they were beautiful to her, as beautiful as a gem skilfully placed by a jeweller. As the Christian reflects upon Christ's caring, discerning eyes, he has to say the same. The eyes of Christ are 'fitly set'. There is no flaw or deficiency in them. What a glorious beloved we have in Christ! Such a glorious Christ calls for our praise and our commitment even as this young woman gave praise and commitment to her beloved.

The cheeks of Christ

The Shulamite continues her description of the beloved by likening his cheeks to 'a bed of spices' and 'banks of scented herbs' (5:13). In his commentary on the Song of Solomon, George Burrowes gives this description of the bed of spices: 'Beside fragrant plants and flowers, the Jewish gardens were occupied, in a considerable degree, with the growth of medicinal shrubs and herbs. The word "bed" here means a bed raised throughout, or at least in the middle; such a plot, thickly covered with sweet-smelling flowers in full bloom, was a most delightful object; and the spouse ... says the pleasure felt by her in gazing on the cheeks of the beloved, could be best illustrated by the delight caused in viewing a bed filled with fragrant flowers.'[1] Concerning the next phrase, 'banks of scented herbs', he continues, 'It seems to mean trellises, and those of a towering height, covered with aromatic flowers.'[2]

Having interpreted the two phrases in this way, Burrowes concludes: 'The whole verse would then read — "His cheeks are as banks or mounds of fragrant flowers, as towering trellises covered with aromatic blooms." '[3]

What is the significance of cheeks? They do not do anything. They are just there. And therein lies their significance. They are receivers. They are passive. One implication of this, when we apply it to Christ, is that he can and does receive affection from his people.

But there is much more to be said at this point. As the cheeks are passive, so there was a passivity about our Lord. Nothing is more beautiful to the people of God than this particular passivity. The truth is, we are saved because of what the Lord Jesus Christ received for us. Old theologians and divines used to distinguish between the active obedience and passive obedience of Christ. The former was the obedience that he actively rendered to the law of God in order to provide the perfect righteousness we need to stand justified before God. The latter referred to the penalty he bore on Calvary's cross in order to pay for our sins. As has often been said, we owed a debt we could not pay; he paid a debt he did not owe.

That passive suffering of Christ is described for us in Isaiah 50, and part of it pertained to his cheeks:

> I gave my back to those who struck me
> And my cheeks to those who plucked out the beard;
> I did not hide my face from shame and spitting
>
> (Isa. 50:6).

Through these two aspects of his obedience, the Lord Jesus Christ did everything necessary for us to have our sins forgiven and to stand clean and guiltless before a holy God.

Do the cheeks represent passivity? I shall ever be thankful to God for the cheeks of Christ, that passivity which took my penalty. Those cheeks will always be as mounds of fragrant flowers to me and towering trellises of aromatic blooms.

The body of Christ

Another aspect of the beauty of the beloved is set forth in the Shulamite's description of his body. She compares it to 'carved ivory inlaid with sapphires' (v. 14).

A reference to the brightness of Solomon's garment

To what does the word translated 'body' refer? Some say it means the whole body. Others translate it 'belly' and say it refers only to the mid-section. Still others translate the word as 'bowels' and say it refers only to the lower portion of the mid-section. But I am inclined to agree with those commentators who take the view that she was referring, not to the body itself, but rather to the beautiful garment that Solomon wore. Stuart Olyott writes, 'The description here is not of the naked person, but of the snow-white robe and girdle, set full of jewels, which were a common feature of royal persons in the Orient.'[4]

The single most impressive quality of this garment would have been its brightness. The whiteness of the garment itself would have made it bright and shining, so that carved and polished ivory would indeed have been a fitting symbol for the bride to use. This brightness would, however, have been further enhanced by decoration with brilliant, blue sapphires. This sparkling, glistening brightness of his body made for a striking and impressive appearance, one that conveyed incredible glory and splendour.

The brightness and glory of the Lord Jesus

Scripture constantly associates brightness with God and heaven (Ezek. 1:4,27-28; 8:2; 10:4; Acts 26:13), but brightness, glory and splendour find their perfect expression in the person of the Lord Jesus Christ. The writer to the Hebrews says Jesus is 'the brightness' of God's glory (Heb. 1:3). In the book of Revelation, the Lord Jesus identifies himself as 'the Bright and Morning Star' (Rev. 22:16).

In other words, the brightness of the glory of God shone in and through the Lord Jesus Christ. The apostle Paul says the 'light of the knowledge of the glory of God' shines 'in the face of Jesus Christ' (2 Cor. 4:6). The apostle John calls Jesus the Word of God, and says of him, 'The Word became flesh and dwelt among us, and we beheld his glory, the glory as of the only begotten of the Father, full of grace and truth' (John 1:14).

What was he saying? Essentially this: as he and the other disciples closely observed and scrutinized the Lord Jesus Christ, they could see flickering through the veil of his humanity the brightness of the glory of God himself. At no time was this shining more clear and apparent than on that day when John accompanied Jesus, along with Peter and James, to a mountain-top. There before their eyes, Jesus was transfigured. Mark describes it in this way: 'His clothes became shining, exceedingly white, like snow, such as no launderer on earth can whiten them' (Mark 9:3). Luke describes the same event: 'As he prayed, the appearance of his face was altered, and his robe became white and glistening' (Luke 9:29).

What did the disciples see on that day? What it amounts to is this: they saw the robe of his humanity pulled aside and their Master clothed in the bright, shining robe of the royalty of the King of kings and Lord of lords. Mark and Luke (and Matthew as well) described the event in terms of brightness and shining, but they could just as easily have taken the words of the Shulamite and spoken of polished ivory adorned with brilliant sapphires. Do we understand this? The Lord Jesus Christ perfectly embodied and expressed the glory of God himself.

Understanding these figures in this way gives us an additional opportunity to stand in awe of our Christ. He who was sparkling with deity and purity stooped low to take our humanity, and in that humanity he went to a bloody death on Calvary. What should our response be to the awesome reality of the glory of God shining in Jesus? Charles Wesley answers:

> Veiled in flesh, the Godhead see,
> Hail the incarnate Deity!

When we see the glory of God in Jesus, the only proper response is to worship him as our God and hail him as our King.

The countenance of Christ

A reference to general appearance

The bride continues to catalogue her beloved's beauty by describing his 'countenance' (5:15), a word we associate with the face. But the Hebrew word translated 'countenance' refers, in the words of Franz Delitsch, to a person's 'look' or 'appearance as a whole'.[5] James Durham agrees: 'Countenance is used in Scripture, not only to signify the face, but the whole stature and presentation of a person, or that which gives a full sight of one in all his parts together ... so it takes in face, legs, body and altogether, when all these are so proportioned, as they make one a person goodly to be seen and looked on... '[6]

The bride is talking, then, about the general appearance of her beloved, and she likens it to the mountainous region of Lebanon. Those mountains were covered with tall, straight, stately cedars. She calls these cedars 'excellent', a word that can be translated 'choice' or 'elect'. The young bride was clearly suggesting that her beloved was the choicest, the most excellent of all men, even as the cedar is the most excellent among trees. The beloved's general appearance was, therefore, of such stateliness and beauty that it placed him apart from all others, in a class by himself.

The beauty of our whole Christ

We should also note that it was the whole man, not just one aspect of him, that caused the bride to praise him as superior to all others. We may apply this to Christ by saying it is the whole Christ that makes him so attractive and delightful to the Christian. We live in a time when many people delight in a partial Christ. They take one aspect of him and exalt it over another. This finds its most frequent expression when they exalt the love and grace of Christ over his holiness and justice.

The true Christian will not be content with a reduced or pruned Christ. Give him the full Christ, with his electing love, his wisdom and power, his justice and grace, his deity and humanity, his perfect atonement, his eternal purpose — and the Christian will delight in each and every part.

5.
The church proclaims his strength

'His locks are wavy, and black as a raven... His hands are rods of gold... His legs are pillars of marble'
(S. of S. 5:11-15).

Some parts of the Shulamite's description of her beloved relate more to his beauty while other parts deal with his strength. What she says about his head, eyes, body and countenance all belongs to the former category. Now we turn our attention to those parts of the description that praise his strength.

It is interesting that the Shulamite found it necessary to use so many figures to describe the beauty and strength of her beloved (5:9). With the phrase 'chief among ten thousand', she drew her metaphor from the military world. Then she turned to the realm of precious materials to talk about her beloved's head and to the birds of the air to describe his hair and eyes. And in describing the latter she included a couple of other images: milk and the skilful work of a jeweller. In verse 13, she enters the world of scents, while the conclusion of her description takes us again to the realm of precious materials (5:14-15) and to the particular loveliness of Lebanon, with its tall, stately cedars (5:15).

It seems that it was no easy thing for this young woman to answer the question of the daughters of Jerusalem: 'What is your beloved more than another beloved?' It appears to have taxed her considerably, to have pressed her to the limit of her descriptive abilities. She seems to be saying, 'I can't answer that question in a quick, easy way. My beloved is not like any-

one else or anything else. I will have to draw on many anal-
ogies to give you an answer, and even then that answer will be
incomplete and inadequate.'

Christians certainly feel this sense of inadequacy when they
have the opportunity to talk about Christ. They feel it when
they come before him in worship and prayer and begin to praise
his glorious attributes. Perhaps we are conscious of a special
sense of inadequacy when it comes to the strength of Christ.
In the bride's description of Solomon's hands, legs and hair
we are able to discern glimmers of the mighty strength of our
Christ.

The hands of Christ

Gold set with beryl

The Shulamite compares the hands of Solomon to 'gold set
with beryl' (5:14). Commentators differ widely on exactly what
she meant by these words. Some take them as a reference to
the gold rings which he wore. Others say she was not referring to the rings on his fingers, but rather to his hands themselves. George Burrowes writes, 'The idea here is, not that his
fingers were covered with golden rings, but that the fingers
were as gold rings, rollers, or cylinders, and the nails were as
the beryl set in those rings.'[1]

Scholars also differ on the meaning of 'beryl'. The word in
the original is 'Tarshish' and may refer to a stone having the
sea-green colour of the Sea of Tarshish. The *Holman Bible
Dictionary* identifies it as 'a light green precious stone closely
related to the emeralds and aquamarines'.[2]

We do know that beryl, whatever its precise identity, was
highly regarded among the ancients. It was one of the precious stones in the breastplate of the high priest (Exod. 28:20),

one of the gems Ezekiel saw in his vision of the wheels (Ezek. 1:16), and it is to be one of the foundation stones of the New Jerusalem (Rev. 21:20). By coupling the gold and the beryl, the Shulamite was obviously saying the hands of her beloved were extremely precious and attractive to her.

I do not know what made the hands of her beloved so beautiful to this young woman. I am sure Solomon's hands were as gloriously adorned as the rest of his person and, in the light of that, the young Shulamite may have found it necessary to resort to these symbols in order to describe them adequately. Or it could be that she was looking beyond the adornment of his hands to what she had experienced from them. Those strong hands that signed the decrees and controlled the various functions of government had no doubt bestowed lavish gifts upon her and had gently and lovingly caressed her. They may have comforted her with a soothing touch when she was despondent. Although I cannot be sure why the hands of Solomon were so exceedingly attractive and compelling to her, I can apply what she says to Christ. No hands are more precious than the hands of the Lord Jesus Christ.

The creative hands of Christ

There are several things I understand about these hands from the Scriptures. I understand that they are powerful hands — so powerful that all creation came from them! God says through the prophet Isaiah:

> I have made the earth,
> And created man on it.
> It was I —
> My hands that stretched out the heavens,
> And all their host I have commanded
>
> (Isa. 45:12).

God also says, 'Indeed my hand has laid the foundation of the earth, and my right hand has stretched out the heavens' (Isa. 48:13).

The psalmist recognized the creative hand of God when he addressed the Lord and said, 'Of old you laid the foundation of the earth, and the heavens are the work of your hands' (Ps. 102:25).

The creative hand of God was also the creative hand of Christ. The apostle John, speaking of Christ, writes, 'He was in the beginning with God. All things were made through him, and without him nothing was made that was made' (John 1:2-3).

Those powerful hands of creation are also the hands that preserve creation. The apostle Paul says of Christ, 'In him all things consist' (Col. 1:17), while Hebrews tells us that Christ is even now 'upholding all things by the word of his power' (Heb. 1:3). The psalms speak of God opening his hand in providential care to provide for earth's creatures (Ps. 104:28; 145:15-16).

Kind and loving hands

The verses just referred to in Psalms 104 and 145 remind us that those powerful hands of creation and preservation are also kind and loving hands. The loving hand of God dispenses deliverance to his people (Ps. 136:12). With that same hand he sustains them by providing for their needs (Ps. 37:24-25). With that hand he holds, as it were, the hands of his people and guides them along (Ps. 73:23; 139:9-10). The Lord's hand also upholds the one who stumbles (Ps. 37:24), and distributes freely and liberally the graces and gifts that the people of God enjoy (Eph. 4:7–16). If Christ is the one who upholds all things, it follows that Christ is the one who supplied, and still supplies, these gracious providences.

Sometimes the hand of God manifests his love for his people by dispensing chastisement to them. David found it to be so. On one occasion he wrote, 'For day and night your hand was heavy upon me; my vitality was turned into the drought of summer' (Ps. 32:4). On another occasion, he prayed, 'Remove your plague from me; I am consumed by the blow of your hand' (Ps. 39:10).

I thank God that Jesus Christ actually had hands — human hands. This tells us that he left the glories of heaven and became one of us. Had the eternal God himself not taken human hands, there would have been absolutely no hope for us. But not only did Christ take human hands, he used those hands. And how he used them! I see them now, lifting up Jairus' daughter (Matt. 9:25). I see them breaking the loaves and fishes for a hungry multitude (John 6:1-14). I see them reaching down to take some clay, mixing it with his own saliva and applying it to the eyes of a blind man (John 9:1-7). I see him extending them towards Lazarus' tomb as he cries out, 'Lazarus, come forth!' (John 11:43).

Most of all, when I think of the hands of Christ, I see a cruel cross. There, those hands that had so kindly and faithfully ministered to others were stretched out and nails were hammered through them. And I understand that this was not just a cruel twist of fate, an unforeseen development, but rather it was the plan of God for dealing with my sins. I understand that Jesus willingly stretched out those hands that day and received those nails that I might be freed from my sins. He took the wrath of God in my stead so that I could be released from that wrath.

Thank God for the precious hands of the Lord Jesus! They are like gold set with beryl to me!

But there is even more. The Scriptures tell me that the hands of Christ are the hands of God and that those hands now firmly hold me, along with all who believe (Ps. 73:23; 139:10; John

10:28-30). John Gill writes, 'Never do the hands of Christ look more beautiful and lovely, than when he is beheld as grasping, holding, and retaining his people in his hands, out of which they can never be plucked.'[3] As we reflect on these things we can see the truth of the psalmist's statement: 'And we are the people of his pasture, and the sheep of his hand' (Ps. 95:7).

The legs of Christ

Pillars, marble, and gold

After describing the hands of her beloved, the bride proceeds to liken his legs to 'pillars of marble set on bases of fine gold' (5:15). This description embodies, or encompasses, three things: pillars, marble and gold. Pillars we associate with orderliness, strength and beauty. Marble is a non-metallic material that we associate with stability and stateliness. Gold we associate with glory and excellence.

What then was this young woman saying about the legs of her beloved? They were quite obviously strong, with fine muscle-tone that gave him a beautiful and stately bearing and gait. The Shulamite's description of the legs of her beloved inevitably causes the Christian to think of his beloved — the Lord Jesus Christ.

First, we may say the legs (instruments of walking) represent the strength and activity of Christ as Saviour; pillars represent the stateliness, orderliness and majesty of his eternal purpose; marble pictures the beauty and stability of his works and ways. That brings us to gold, which represents the glory and excellence of his divine person. Let us look further at the strength of Christ.

Christ the load-bearer

When we assemble all these metaphors and relate them to Christ, here is what we come up with: he is a strong Christ (able to bear the burden or the load placed on him), and all his ways are stable, orderly and beautiful.

Have you ever thought about Christ having to bear a load? What about the load of government? In his prophecy on the coming of Christ, Isaiah tells us, 'The government will be upon his shoulder' (Isa. 9:6). What is this government? Is it not the government of the whole universe? Speaking of Christ the apostle Paul writes, 'For by him all things were created that are in heaven and that are on earth, visible and invisible, whether thrones or dominions or principalities or powers. All things were created through him and for him. And he is before all things, and in him all things consist' (Col. 1:16-17). All things 'consist' in Christ. That means he holds all things together. The government, or management, of all things has been committed to him.

In addition to the burden of government, there was the load of redemption. What was this load? It was the load of the sins of those he died to redeem. Isaiah stresses this in his prophecy of Christ's redeeming death on the cross. He speaks of Christ as bearing our griefs (53:4), carrying our sorrows (53:4) and bearing our iniquities and sins (53:11–12). He also says that 'The Lord has laid on him the iniquity of us all' (53:6).

What a frightful burden this was! It was a load we could not carry ourselves. God has decreed that the penalty for sin is separation from him for ever, and there was absolutely no way we could be freed from the crushing burden of sin by ourselves. But Christ took our load. There on the cross, he bore in his own person that penalty of separation from God, which for us would have been an eternal separation. Now that Christ has paid the penalty for our sins, there is no penalty left for us to pay and we are enabled to go free.

How we should praise God for the strong legs of Christ that were able to bear up under that crushing load of guilt and sin! Isn't it fascinating that when the Lord Jesus Christ bore our penalty on Calvary's cross the Roman soldiers broke the legs of the two thieves crucified with him, but they did not break his legs? (John 19:32-33). What a fitting testimony to those strong legs! They were never broken, not even when the burden of our sin had crushed him in death!

What strength there is in our Christ! That strength is often captured in the word 'able'. How sweet that word is when it is applied to Christ! The author of Hebrews uses it. He tells us that Christ 'is ... able to save to the uttermost those who come to God through him' (Heb. 7:25). The same author also says Christ is 'able to aid' his people when they are tempted (Heb. 2:18). The little epistle of Jude also uses that word 'able' in connection with the Lord. It says he is 'able' to keep God's people from stumbling and present them 'faultless' before 'the presence of his glory' (Jude 24).

It occurs to me, finally, that strong legs can trample down as well as bear up. There on the cross, Christ trampled sin, Satan and death and defeated them all. But Scripture solemnly warns us that there is more trampling to come. Those who do not cast themselves on the mercy of Christ, who carried the load of redemption for sinners, will find that same strong Christ trampling them in judgement.

Christ's providential care

In addition to representing strength to carry a load, the legs also represent a person's walk or deportment. Here we deal with our Lord's providential dealings with his people. In addition to the general government of all things, and the burden of sin that he bore for his elect, Christ has in particular the government of his people. John Gill says this involves 'their burdens ... their trials, temptations, and afflictions'.⁴ The prophet Isaiah ridiculed the idolaters of his day for worshipping a god they had to carry around. He says:

> They bear it on the shoulder, they carry it
> And set it in its place, and it stands;
> From its place it shall not move.
> Though one cries out to it, yet it cannot answer
> Nor save him out of his trouble
>
> (Isa. 46:7).

Isaiah was glad to declare that God's people did not have to carry their God. He carried them! The Lord says:

> Listen to me, O house of Jacob,
> And all the remnant of the house of Israel,
> Who have been upheld by me from birth,
> Who have been carried from the womb:
> Even to your old age, I am he,
> And even to grey hairs I will carry you!
> I have made, and I will bear;
> Even I will carry, and will deliver you
>
> (Isa. 46:3-4).

Idolatry is more sophisticated today than it was in those days, but it is still very much with us. Pleasure, position, possessions, power — these are just some of the false gods of this day. Multitudes chase madly after them and serve them. But sooner or later life brings us to that point at which we need to be carried, and the devotees of these gods are face to face with the stark reality that their gods are unable to carry them. Their gods are a load, not a lift. The Christian finds his Lord to be just the opposite: he is a lift, not a load.

While Christians rejoice in the strength of the load-carrying Christ, they oftentimes find themselves perplexed and mystified about the way he orders their circumstances. Many Christians, if pressed on this point, would say the load-carrying legs of Christ are strong, but the way-walking legs of Christ are sometimes strange.

We should not expect to be able to understand fully the ways of the Lord. He plainly tells us that his thoughts are not our thoughts and his ways are not our ways (Isa. 55:8). Yet we persist in thinking that God should do things the way we want them done. Even though we cannot fully understand the ways of God, we can, through his Word, understand the overarching purpose behind them. Paul says, 'And we know that all things work together for good to those who love God, to those who are the called according to his purpose' (Rom. 8:28).

The Lord has, then, the best interests of his children at heart in all his ways. Our profound need is to trust that this is true even when it does not seem to be true. What we call the strangeness of God's ways could be more accurately called the smallness of our faith.

The black hair of Christ

Yet another indication of her beloved's strength is mentioned by the Shulamite early in her description, namely, his hair. She notes the waviness, or abundance, and blackness of it (5:11). These features must certainly be taken as emblems of his youthful strength and vigour. We associate grey hair, or the absence of hair, with advancing years, but her beloved wore the abundant, black hair of youthfulness. Does the beloved's hair indicate the vigour and vitality of the prime of life? Then we must say that Christ is the perfect expression of such vigour and vitality.

Some may think it is wrong to use the black hair of the beloved as an emblem of the Lord Jesus. They remember the vision of the apostle John in the book of Revelation. There the Lord is represented as having hair 'white like wool, as white as snow' (Rev. 1:14). Do we contradict that verse when we say Christ has black hair? No. The white hair of Revelation tells us Christ is old, as old as eternity. But here lies the greatness of our Christ. Even though he is as old as eternity itself, he has lost none of his power or vigour. Even though he is old, he is for ever young. The author of Hebrews affirms this truth by saying, 'Jesus Christ is the same yesterday, today, and for ever' (Heb. 13:8). There is no deterioration or decay in Christ.

Of this glorious truth, James Durham writes, 'Christ's perfections are continuing perfections; he is a Beloved that never decays, that never waxeth sick, weak, nor old; but is ever in youth, with his hair black, although he be eternal, and the Ancient of days, for all his properties are unchangeably in him, and ever agree to him ... this is good and very comfortable to his people; Christ sets not up nor fails; his Spouse weeps not for the death, decays, or waxing old of her Beloved and Husband, which can be said of no other.'⁵

Durham is certainly correct in saying, 'This is good and very comfortable to his people.' Because Christ is ever vigorous and strong and incapable of decay, we can trust him to uphold us and help us for time and eternity. We may apply to Christ these words:

> For this is God,
> Our God for ever and ever;
> He will be our guide
> Even to death.

(Ps. 48:14).

This brings us to the conclusion of the Shulamite's detailed description of her beloved, a description in which she gladly and enthusiastically proclaimed his excellence. The church of Christ has been charged with the task of proclaiming the excellence of her Christ. As we have worked our way through the Shulamite's description, we have seen Christ at every turn, and we have been made to realize what a glorious Christ we have to proclaim. He is sovereign in majesty, constant and unchanging, tender and compassionate. He shines with deity and glory. He supplies the needs of his people. He is the strong Christ who bears the loads of government and redemption. He is the Christ who passively received the wrath of God in the stead of his people.

All of these things should make us marvel at our Christ. They should also make us marvel that it is possible these days to hear very little of Christ in many churches. Is it not a startling thing that the church should be silent about such a glorious Christ? May God help us to see his excellence again and give ourselves wholeheartedly both to knowing and to proclaiming it.

Section II

The experience of the believer

6.
The kisses of Christ

'Let him kiss me with the kisses of his mouth — for your love is better than wine' (S. of S.1:2).

As we have noted previously, most of the Song of Solomon consists of the words of the Shulamite or those of her beloved, as she speaks to him and he responds to her. It is a song of mutual love, and love thrives on loving exchanges and mutual praise.

These loving exchanges come very quickly in the Song. It begins abruptly with the bride acknowledging her strong desire to be kissed by her beloved. The kiss is, of course, a manifestation of love, of the tenderest affection. In desiring her beloved's kisses, the bride was seeking an enormous privilege. After all, her beloved was the great and wise Solomon, the King of Israel. It was considered to be a high honour for the king even to extend his hand and allow one of his citizens to kiss it. But the Shulamite is expressing something completely unthinkable — that is, the desire to be kissed by the king! And not just one kiss will do! She desires 'the kisses of his mouth'. All the kisses he has to offer, she wants to receive.

Note further that she admits this desire to the king himself. It is evident that she is speaking to him because she adds: 'For your love is better than wine' (1:2). The shift from the third person ('him' in the first line of the verse) to the second person ('your' in the second line) may be explained in this way: the bride, speaking to her beloved, begins by telling him what had been going through her mind ('Let him kiss me'), and then tells him why she had been thinking this ('Your love is better than wine').

What does the Shulamite's desire for the kisses of her beloved have to do with us? Many would not hesitate to say it has nothing at all, or very little, to contribute to our experience of Christ. As far as they are concerned, this is nothing more than mere history couched in poetry, and its only function is to remind us of the beauty of such love and to hold before us the ideal that we should all be striving for in our marriages.

But Scripture entitles us to say there is much more here than mere romance. In fact it frequently uses the metaphor of the kiss to reflect the joys of the Christian's relationship to Christ.

The kiss of Calvary

As we examine the Scriptures on this matter, we are first constrained to say that the Christian owes his very salvation to certain kisses. One of the psalms speaks of the satisfying of both justice and grace, in terms of kissing: 'Mercy and truth have met together; righteousness and peace have kissed...' (Ps. 85:10).

Could there possibly be a better description of what happened on the cross? There God's justice, truth and righteousness met with his grace, mercy and peace, and they kissed. They were completely reconciled and satisfied.

Every Christian knows that this salvation can only be attributed to Christ's atoning death on Calvary's cross. But what is the meaning of the cross? What did Christ do there? What was there about his death that made it possible for our sins to be forgiven and for us to receive title to eternal glory?

Some argue that Christ died only to demonstrate the love of God for us. We ought to look at what he did there for us, feel ashamed of ourselves for being the way we are, and resolve to do better. The cross, according to this view, was designed only to exert a moral influence on us. But there was much, much more to it than that! Christ was crucified on Golgotha's hill, if I may put it in this way, because of a sharp dilemma — God's dilemma. That dilemma may be summarized in this way: how could God punish sin and yet pardon the sinner? Or, to use Paul's phrase, how could God be both 'just and the justifier'? (Rom. 3:26). How could God retain his justice while justifying guilty sinners?

God's justice demanded that the sentence he had pronounced against sinners be carried out, the sentence of eternal separation from himself. But God is also a God of grace, and his grace pleaded for mercy for the sinner. The cross of Christ represents the solution to that dilemma. There, both justice and grace were satisfied. Justice was satisfied because sin was punished in the person of Christ. God actually poured out on his Son an eternity of wrath, so justice had no more to say. But grace was satisfied there as well. Since Christ bore the penalty of God against sin for his people, there is no more penalty for them to pay. Jesus has paid it, and justice cannot demand that it be paid a second time. Since Christ has paid the ransom price, those who rely completely on his atoning work are free.

The kiss of reconciliation

There is no more glorious picture of reconciliation than our Lord's parable of the prodigal son. That son, like all of us, rebelled against his father and went into the far country. He was alienated from his father as hostility and resentment ran at flood-tide in his heart. But the son was enabled to see his folly, and he made his way home. As he journeyed he carefully rehearsed what he would say to his father: 'Father, I have sinned against heaven and before you, and I am no longer worthy to be called your son. Make me like one of your hired servants' (Luke 15:18-19).

In some of the most dramatic and moving words in all of Scripture, Jesus brings the parable to a glorious climax: 'And he arose and came to his father. But when he was still a great way off, his father saw him and had compassion, and ran and fell on his neck and kissed him' (Luke 15:20). Here we have the kiss of reconciliation. Alienation and separation were ended. Rebellion and hostility were gone. The son was home and the father and son were reconciled.

In this moving story we have a powerful picture of the sinner coming to God the Father. And when he comes, he is received and kissed with the kiss of reconciliation. The apostle Paul writes, 'Now all things are of God, who has reconciled us to himself through Jesus Christ' (2 Cor. 5:18).

As a result of Christ's death on the cross, the sinner can be received by God the Father and reconciled to him. We must be clear at this point. While we are in our sins, we are alienated from God. We are his enemies. Yes, sin is that serious. It is enmity against God. It is the creature thumbing his nose at his Creator and saying, 'I refuse to acknowledge you as my Creator and refuse to order my life according to your law.'

The cross, and that alone, can remove this hostility and enmity. The Holy Spirit of God speaks to the heart of the sinner, causing him to become aware of God and of what God is like. He further enables him to see his dreadful state of rebellion and the impending judgement of the God he has opposed. But the Holy Spirit also points to that cross of Christ as the solution to the problem. He tells the sinner that he no longer has to live in rebellion and in fear of judgement, that Jesus Christ's death is sufficient even for him, and that God the Father stands ready now to receive him on the basis of that death.

The Holy Spirit not only enlightens the mind to understand these things, he also woos the sinner to embrace them. He elevates the affections, so that the sinner now sees eternal salvation, and the cross that provides it, as his highest good. The Spirit also energizes the will, so the sinner is able to repent of his sins and lay hold upon 'Christ and him crucified' in believing faith. Thus the sinner throws down his weapons of rebellion and comes with brokenness and sorrow into the presence of the heavenly Father, saying:

> Nothing in my hand I bring,
> Simply to thy cross I cling.
>
> (Augustus M. Toplady)

And, wonder of wonders, the heavenly Father gladly receives him. The enmity and hostility are over. Peace has been made. God and sinner are reconciled.

The kiss of the gospel ministry

The Bible has still more to say about kisses. The marvellous kisses we have just noted are made known to us through the gospel ministry. Paul talked about receiving 'the ministry of reconciliation', the declaration that 'God was in Christ reconciling the world to himself' (2 Cor. 5:18,19). If God's reception of the sinner can be likened to a kiss of reconciliation, it stands to reason that the ministry of reconciliation can also be likened to a kiss. But there is an even stronger evidence for comparing the gospel ministry to a kiss. One of Solomon's proverbs says, 'He who gives a right answer kisses the lips' (Prov. 24:26).

When we stop to consider the sinner's terrible plight —
estranged from God through sin and under the sentence of
eternal wrath — there can certainly be no doubt that the good
news of reconciliation through Christ is the 'right answer'.
We must not miss the contrast that Solomon draws at this
point. Not all give the right answer. Some say to the wicked:
'You are righteous' (Prov. 24:24).

This forces us to face a most distasteful and unsavoury fact.
Not all ministers are true. Some do not give the right answer.
The right answer is reconciliation to God through Christ, but
some tell their hearers they have nothing to be concerned about.
There is no need for reconciliation to God, they say, because
men are already acceptable to him by nature. These ministers
ignore sin and consequently ignore the cross as God's solution for sin. They preach peace when there is no peace (Jer.
4:10; 6:14). Such ministers may seem to be offering a pleasant
kiss, but in reality it is a curse.

> He who says to the wicked, 'You are righteous,'
> Him the people will curse;
> Nations will abhor him.
> But those who rebuke the wicked will have delight,
> And a good blessing will come upon them
> > (Prov. 24:24-25).

How we should prize the ministry that tells us the truth
about our sin and points us to Christ!

The kisses of the Christian life

The Christian definitely finds the kisses of Christ in the reconciling work of Christ and the gospel ministry that informs him
of it, but that is just the beginning. As the Christian walks with

his Lord, he finds there are many more such kisses. The kiss is, of course, a manifestation of love, and the Christian life is filled with such manifestations, experiences which James Durham refers to as 'sensible manifestations' of his love.[1]

Have you not, child of God, experienced these? Can you not point to times when Christ suddenly and inexplicably drew you near to himself and gave you the inner realization that you belong to him and that he loves you in a special way? Perhaps it was while you were reading from the Word of God. Or it may have been while you were engaged in prayer, or while you were singing a hymn, or listening to a sermon in public worship. Or it may have happened when you were not even engaged in religious exercises at all, but you were suddenly made aware of Christ's incredible love for you. Suddenly, the truth and the glory of it all just overwhelmed you. You were made to realize that Christ has loved you and died for you, that he now prizes you as his own dear possession, and that he is finally going to take you to himself to share his unspeakable glory.

Every Christian can recall such kisses, those times when he was overwhelmed with a sense of the wonder and glory of it all, times when he realized afresh how guilty and undeserving he was, and yet the Lord of glory had reached down to the pit of his condemnation, plucked him out, and made him an heir to his eternal glory. Every time the Christian is made to feel the tender affection the Saviour has for him, he has, in effect, been kissed by Christ.

As the Christian learns about these kisses, he comes to desire them earnestly, even as the Shulamite longed for the kisses of Solomon. But the believer also finds himself desiring the kiss of God's blessing upon his service. He desires the kiss of God's presence in his worship. He desires the kiss of God's comfort in his trials. He desires the kiss of God's guidance when he is confused. He desires the kiss of God's sustaining care when he is weary. He desires the kiss of God's forgiveness when he sins. He desires the kiss of God's assurance when he doubts. He desires the kiss of God's provision when his future looks bleak. He looks forward to that glorious day when Christ will return and kiss the bodies of all dead believers with the kiss of his resurrection power.

What does it mean when something like this happens to us? It means we have been kissed by the Lord Jesus! And when it happens, we must readily agree with the bride in the Song of Solomon by saying it is the sweetest thing on this earth.

The kisses bestowed on Christ

As we explore the Scriptures on this matter of kissing, we soon realize the Christian has not only been kissed by Christ, but also that he kisses Christ in return. Kissing is reciprocal in nature. One of the most loved portions of the Song of Solomon is the bride's detailed description of her beloved (5:10-16). Each part of this description may be applied to the Lord Jesus Christ. Some of the details are more easily applied to Christ than others and there is no difficulty, for instance, with the head and the hands.

But what about his cheeks? What possible connection is there between what the bride says about the cheeks of her beloved and the Christian's beloved? As I turned that question over in my mind, it occurred to me that cheeks are receivers. They do not do anything, but they often receive a kiss or a caress. Should not the cheeks of the Shulamite's beloved speak to us, then, about the affection, the kisses, that Christ is to receive from his people?

In his powerful sermon on the cheeks of the beloved, 'Spices, Flowers, Lilies, and Myrrh', Charles Spurgeon says, 'The cheek is the place of fellowship where we exchange tokens of love. What a blessing it is that Christ should have had a cheek for the lips of love to approach, and to kiss! What a privilege it is that ever it should be possible for a loving heart to express its affection to Christ!'[2] What are these kisses the Christian bestows upon the Lord? Let us see.

The kiss of trembling submission

This first kiss is presented by the psalmist in these words:

> Kiss the Son, lest he be angry,
> And you perish in the way,
> When his wrath is kindled but a little.
> Blessed are all those who put their trust in him
>
> (Ps. 2:12).

These words constitute the psalmist's wise counsel to men who are filled with anxiety, even to the point that they are compared to the tossing and raging sea (Ps. 2:1). In their feverish anxiety, they rush together for consultation on how to remove the cause of their agitation. And what is the cause of it all? The psalmist leaves us in no doubt. It is 'the Lord' and 'his anointed'. In other words, these men want to be free from God and his anointed king. Who is this anointed king? He is none other than the Messiah, the Lord Jesus Christ. These men do not want to be fettered by God's commands. They want to be their own gods.

And what is God's response to all their ranting and raving? Is he stricken with terror? Does he fly into a panic? Does he call an emergency session of the heavenly cabinet? Hardly. The psalmist says he laughs. He scoffs at puny men as they strut briefly across the stage of history, shaking their fists in his face and fuming at him (Ps. 2:4). After he laughs at these men, God speaks to them: 'Yet I have set my King on my holy hill of Zion' (Ps. 2:6). With these words, the sovereign God declares that what his enemies are trying to prevent is already an accomplished fact. Christ has already been made King, and nothing can prevent it or nullify it. Spurgeon sums it up in these words: 'While they are proposing, he has disposed the matter. Jehovah's will is done, and man's will frets and raves in vain. God's Anointed is appointed, and shall not be disappointed.'[3]

So hostility against God and his Son is futile. What is left then? The psalmist's counsel — kiss the Son! Recognize the sovereign decree of God that Jesus Christ is King, throw down the arms of rebellion and, as any wise subject would do, bow before him in true homage and affection. Those who refuse to take their place as humble subjects of their rightful King can expect this King to do what any king would do — destroy them as rebels. The choice, then, is clear: bow as a subject to Christ, or perish as a rebel.

> Ye sinners seek his grace
> Whose wrath ye cannot bear;
> Fly to the shelter of his cross,
> And find salvation there.
>
> (Anon.)

The Christian has, by the grace of God, kissed the King. He has seen the folly of rebellion against the one who must rule and will rule. He has cast aside his weapons, and with a heart filled with awe and affection he has taken his place before the king in trembling and glad submission.

The kiss of gratitude bestowed on Christ

Let the sinful woman in Luke 7 speak to us about the kiss of gratitude. This woman came to Jesus while he was having supper with Simon the Pharisee and kissed, not his cheeks, but his feet, washed them with her tears, and anointed them with fragrant oil. Simon was shocked that Jesus would allow such a sinful woman even to approach him. But Jesus understood. Her kisses flowed from a heart overwhelmed with gratitude. Although a vile sinner, she had found abounding mercy. As far as she was concerned, the only fitting response to mercy full and free was kisses of gratitude (Luke 7:36-50).

We cannot wash the feet of Christ and kiss them. But we can bestow kisses of gratitude on him. When we gather together to praise his name and exalt his salvation, or when we come before his throne of grace in prayer to thank him and adore him, we plant kisses of affection on his cheek. What is the observance of the Lord's Supper except an occasion for us to kiss the cheek of Christ?

Are we, in fact, bestowing these kisses on Christ? They flow from a heart of love. But the sad reality is that our love towards Christ can abate (Matt. 24:12). The church of Ephesus will for ever stand as a lasting reminder of the tragedy of love grown cold. There was much in that church to commend: sound doctrine, concern about holiness, energetic service — all existed in the church of Ephesus. But there was something missing — the fervent love for Christ they had known at first (Rev. 2:1-7).

The kiss of fellowship bestowed on fellow believers

As we read the Word of God, we discover that there is yet another kiss for the Christian to bestow — that is, the kiss of fellowship upon his brothers and sisters in Christ (1 Cor. 16:20; 2 Cor. 13:12; 1 Thess. 5:26; 1 Peter 5:14). In some cultures, this kiss of fellowship is still expressed by an actual kiss on the cheek. In cultures such as our own, it is expressed in warm handshakes and embraces, in deeds of kindness and in expressions of appreciation and concern. Any way in which a believer expresses love for another Christian may be considered a kiss of fellowship.

Such love is inevitable. The apostle John puts it bluntly: 'If someone says, "I love God," and hates his brother, he is a liar; for he who does not love his brother whom he has seen, how can he love God whom he has not seen? And this commandment we have from him; that he who loves God must love his brother also' (1 John 4:20-21).

7.
Christq the shepherd

'Tell me, O you whom I love, where you feed your flock...'
(S. of S.1:7-8).

Have you ever wondered how King Solomon met a Shulamite shepherdess and began a romance with her? It is extremely doubtful whether such a young woman would have had any occasion to be in the king's court at Jerusalem. Solomon evidently owned a vineyard near where she lived (8:11) and probably came to the area to visit it.

Perhaps it was while he was making his way there that this young woman caught his eye, and he determined to meet her. But not wanting to overwhelm her with all the trappings of royalty, he decided to disguise himself as a shepherd, and the young woman, taken in by his ruse, asked where he kept his flock (1:7). She wanted to know where he was planning to feed and rest his sheep so she could join him later. She did not want to have to wander from flock to flock looking for him. She was apparently afraid some evil would befall her if she were forced to wander among the other shepherds.

Solomon's response seems to have been of a teasing nature. His 'flock' was nowhere to be seen, but he suggested that she follow their tracks and look for the shepherds' tents (1:8). His playful ruse evidently did not last very long, for we soon find the Shulamite speaking of him as the king (1:12). Solomon's posing as a shepherd and the Shulamite's enquiry about his flock open the door for us to consider the Lord Jesus Christ as a shepherd. Solomon may have only pretended to be a shepherd, but the Lord Jesus Christ is a shepherd in every sense of the word.

Christ the Shepherd prophesied

There is a considerable body of Scripture that presents Christ as the Shepherd of his people. Old Testament passages anticipate his tender care for his flock. The prophet Isaiah says:

> He will feed his flock like a shepherd;
> He will gather the lambs with his arm,
> And carry them in his bosom,
> And gently lead those who are with young
>
> (Isa. 40:11).

These words refer to God's actions in shepherding his people by bringing them out of captivity in the land of Babylon and restoring them to their own land. Similar imagery is found in Jeremiah 31:10 and Ezekiel 34:8-31. But we do no violence to these passages if we see them stretching far beyond the immediate historical situation to speak of the Lord Jesus. I say that for the following reasons:

1. Jesus himself encourages us to do so by assuring us that everything we find in Scripture pertains to him (Luke 24:27,44).
2. The New Testament writers had no hesitation in relating these passages to Christ. In each of these Old Testament chapters we find verses that are clearly connected to Christ by New Testament authors (Matthew 3:3 quotes Isaiah 40:3 and Matthew 2:18 quotes Jeremiah 31:15). We are entitled, therefore, to view all

of Isaiah 40 and Jeremiah 31 from a Christological perspective.

We can have no doubts at all about whether the words of Ezekiel 34:23 apply to Christ: 'I will establish one shepherd over them, and he shall feed them — my servant David. He shall feed them and be their shepherd.' This prophecy makes it clear that the coming Messiah would rise from the line of David and also that he would fulfil the promise God had made to David that his house and kingdom would be established for ever (2 Sam. 7:16).

Nor can there be any doubt that the following words from the prophet Micah look to Christ:

And he shall stand and feed his flock
In the strength of the LORD,
In the majesty of the name of the LORD his God;
And they shall abide,
For now he shall be great
To the ends of the earth…

(Micah 5:4).

The context of this prophecy makes it indisputable that it refers to Christ. A few verses earlier, in Micah 5:2, the village of Bethlehem is named as the birthplace of 'the one to be ruler in Israel, whose goings forth have been from of old, from everlasting'. Such words can only refer to Christ.

But notice the content of the prophecy. The Lord Jesus would come to be the ruler in Israel, but he would rule by standing among his people and feeding his flock 'in the strength of the LORD, in the majesty of the name of the LORD his God'. And this feeding would result in their abiding in him. Those who are ruled by Christ manifest it by continuing in submission to him and faith in him.

Through the inspiration of God's Spirit, the Old Testament prophets anticipated a Messiah who would be like a shepherd to God's people. When the Lord Jesus came on the scene, their prophecies were fulfilled to the letter. The Gospel of Mark notes his shepherd's heart in these words: 'And Jesus, when he came out, saw a great multitude and was moved with compassion for them, because they were like sheep not having a shepherd. So he began to teach them many things' (Mark 6:34).

That shepherd's heart was on view each time he opened blind eyes or deaf ears or caused the lame to walk. It was on display when he cast out demons and raised the dead. It was demonstrated when he engaged sin-weary souls in earnest conversation and pointed them to himself as the only answer to their need.

Christ purchasing his sheep

Most of all, that shepherd's heart was on display when Jesus went to Calvary's cross and laid down his life for his sheep. In the tenth chapter of his Gospel, the apostle John records Jesus speaking at length about this very matter. Four times in this passage Jesus declares that he was going to 'give' or 'lay down' his life for his sheep (John 10:11,15,17,18).

It was not often that concern for the sheep caused a shepherd to lose his own life. The best-known shepherd of the Old Testament, David, put his life on the line for his sheep at least twice — once when they were threatened by a bear and once when a lion attacked them, but in each instance David was able to defend his sheep and save his own life. However, in the case of Jesus it was different. The salvation of his flock demanded the sacrifice of his own life. The very fact that the Bible refers to Christ's people as sheep tells us why it was necessary for him to lay down his life. Sheep are defenceless and helpless. Horses kick. Dogs bite. Cats scratch. Snakes strike. Skunks spray. Even turtles have a defence — they hide. But what can sheep do? Nothing.

In this matter of atoning for sin and attaining spiritual life, Christ's sheep were absolutely helpless (Rom. 5:6). The only way Jesus, the Shepherd, could secure life for his sheep was by laying down his own life. He had to absorb the penalty of death in their stead so that they could go free. God 'made him who knew no sin to be sin for us, that we might become the righteousness of God in him' (2 Cor. 5:21).

Christ's death was, therefore, substitutionary in nature. He died 'for the sheep' (John 10:11). His death was instead of their death. Something was about to strike the sheep, but he came between them and the danger and was stricken in their place. Specifically, he absorbed the blow of God's justice against the sins of his people, and in doing so has reconciled us to God (1 Peter 2:24). The apostle Peter summarizes it in this way: 'For you were like sheep going astray, but have now returned to the Shepherd and Overseer of your souls' (1 Peter 2:25).

In addition to being substitutionary, the death of Christ was also voluntary. When Jesus died on the cross his enemies thought they were taking his life from him, but nothing could have been further from the truth. There on the cross the Lord was voluntarily laying his life down to purchase the redemption of his flock. When the Roman procurator, Pilate, accorded to himself too large a role in the crucifixion, the Lord Jesus quickly set the record straight: 'You could have no power at all against me', he said, 'unless it had been given you from above' (John 19:11).

The Lord Jesus also emphasized the victorious nature of his death for his sheep. When Joseph of Arimathea took the body of Jesus and placed it in his own tomb, the enemies of Christ thought they were finally finished with him. They thought

the crucifixion was the last word about Jesus. But the Lord
Jesus went to the cross knowing he would rise from the dead.
Thus he declared that he was laying his life down that he might
'take it again' (John 10:17-18). If Jesus had just died, his death
would have had no value for the sheep. By rising again he
declared that he had justified his sheep (Rom. 4:25), and guaranteed that he would ascend to the Father and send the Holy
Spirit to apply the benefits of his death.

Then there is the co-operative nature of his death. Jesus
makes mention of his Father a total of four times in his 'Good
Shepherd' discourse (John 10:15,17,18). His death was not
something he did on his own. It was part of the plan worked
out with his Father before the world began. And the Father
took special delight in seeing his Son work out, in minute detail and on the stage of history, what they had so carefully
planned together in eternity.

The author of Hebrews tells us that Jesus shed 'the blood
of the everlasting covenant' (Heb. 13:20). The price he paid
to purchase his sheep was not a surprise or an afterthought
with him or with his Father, but was in compliance with the
plan of redemption that they agreed upon before the foundation of the world (2 Tim. 1:9).

Finally, the Lord emphasized the effectiveness of his death
by calling attention to the 'other sheep' he had which were
outside 'this fold' (John 10:16). This meant that his death was
going to reach far beyond the narrow confines of the Jewish
nation and include all the nations of the earth. To see how
powerful and effective the death of Jesus is, we have only to
look at the final book of the Bible. There we find a vast throng
gathered around the throne of God, singing these words to
Christ:

You are worthy to take the scroll,
And to open its seals;

For you were slain,
And have redeemed us to God by your blood
Out of every tribe and tongue and people and nation
(Rev. 5:9).

When we grasp something of the meaning of the death of Christ, we shall understand why the author of Hebrews referred to Jesus as 'that great Shepherd of the sheep' (Heb. 13:20).

Christ tending his sheep

There is much more to being a shepherd, however, than merely purchasing a flock. Sheep have to be fed and watered. They have to be guided and properly rested. They have to be protected from predators, and sometimes from other shepherds. The Lord purchased his flock by his death on Calvary's cross, and he now provides for them.

The Lord Jesus feeds his sheep through under-shepherds. He is the Chief Shepherd (1 Peter 5:4), and he has appointed these under-shepherds to serve the needs of the flock at his direction and under his authority. These under-shepherds are to care for the sheep willingly and lovingly (1 Peter 5:2). They are to feed the sheep with the food the Lord has designated, namely the wholesome, nourishing food of the Word of God.

In his message to the Ephesian elders about feeding the Lord's sheep, the apostle Paul sets out his own example in these words: 'I have not shunned to declare to you the whole counsel of God' (Acts. 20:27). There is the charge given to every under-shepherd: 'Declare the whole counsel of God!' Only then can the sheep grow healthy and strong. Paul later calls this spiritual food 'the word of his grace, which is able to build you up and give you an inheritance among all those who are sanctified' (Acts 20:32). But it is not enough for the under-shepherds to declare that word. They must also exemplify it. They are, in the words of the apostle Peter, not to be 'lords' over those entrusted to them, but rather 'examples to the flock' (1 Peter 5:3).

We surely cannot think about all this without our minds gravitating towards that best-loved of all Scriptures, Psalm 23. The psalm divides quite naturally into two parts. In verses 1-4 David talks about the Lord as his shepherd. In verses 5-6 David talks about the Lord as his host. The section on the Lord as his shepherd can itself be divided into two parts. First, David talks about the Lord's shepherdly care in life (vv.1-3) and then in death (v. 4).

The Lord's care in this life is a combination of tenderness and firmness. The tenderness comes out as David speaks of green pastures and still waters. The Lord does indeed provide for all our needs. But the Shepherd also wants us to conduct ourselves in the right way, and here is where the firmness comes in. When we begin to stray he pulls us back into the way and, in so doing, leads us in paths of righteousness.

From that point David goes on to assert that the Lord's care is sufficient for us in death. Have you ever noticed the shift that takes place in this verse? Up to this point David talks *about* God, but here he begins talking *to* God. He pictures death as entering a valley and confronting a shadow. Suddenly he becomes aware of the fact that someone else is there with him. It is the very same Lord who shepherded him all through life.

This Shepherd, whom David greatly loved, has never been seen during life. But David sees him now, and he sees him clearly enough to discern that he is carrying a rod and staff. The shepherd's rod and staff were sources of much comfort to his sheep. They could be used to rescue sheep from pits and ravines as well as to ward off predators. And David, as he sees them, suddenly finds comfort flooding into his soul. He knew that, as a child of God, he had dreadful enemies, sworn to destroy his soul, but the sight of that rod and that staff brought home the realization that he was absolutely safe. No evil power could touch him, not even death itself.

Many Christians, when they come to the valley of the shadow of death, find themselves beset by the enemies of doubt and guilt. David urges each one to find strength by looking for that great Shepherd of the sheep, there in the shadows. He is more than sufficient to drive away all the enemies that gather around his people at the hour of death.

The separating Shepherd

It is marvellous indeed to reflect on the rich truths Scripture presents under the imagery of Christ as the Shepherd of his people. But the Lord himself also used this same imagery to deliver a very solemn message indeed. He speaks of a day when he will be the separating Shepherd. He says, 'When the Son of Man comes in his glory, and all the holy angels with him, then he will sit on the throne of his glory. All the nations will be gathered before him, and he will separate them one from another, as a shepherd divides his sheep from the goats. And he will set the sheep on his right hand, but the goats on the left. Then the King will say to those on his right hand, "Come you blessed of my Father, inherit the kingdom prepared for you from the foundation of the world..." Then he will also say to those on the left hand, "Depart from me, you cursed, into the everlasting fire prepared for the devil and his angels" ' (Matt. 25:31-34).

The testimony of Scripture is powerful and clear. Those who do not cast themselves totally upon Jesus Christ and rely unreservedly upon his atoning death for their acceptance with

God will find themselves the objects of his wrath, not his
shepherdly care.

> There's a great day coming,
> A great day coming,
> There's a great day coming by and by;
> When the saints and the sinners
> Shall be parted right and left.
> Are you ready for that day to come?...
>
> There's a sad day coming,
> A sad day coming,
> There's a sad day coming by and by;
> When the sinner shall hear his doom,
> 'Depart, I know you not!'
> Are you ready for that day to come?
>
>   (Will L. Thompson).

8.
With Christ in the banqueting hall

'He brought me to the banqueting house, and his banner over me was love...' (S. of S. 2:4).

In Song of Solomon 2:2-3 we find the bridegroom and the bride speaking to each other. The bridegroom says that in comparison to other women his bride is 'like a lily among thorns' (2:2). She responds by saying he is to other men as an apple tree is to all the other trees of the woods. This mutual praise is followed by a distinct shift, which is signalled by the use of the pronoun 'he'. The bride has ceased speaking *to* the bridegroom and has begun speaking *about* him. Verse 7 identifies those to whom she speaks as the 'daughters of Jerusalem'.

Who are these 'daughters of Jerusalem'? We have to answer that question on two levels. On the surface, if the Song is treated as a celebration of the mutual love of Solomon and his bride, they were probably her bridesmaids, or attendants. But on the deeper level, in which the Song pictures the mutual love of Christ and the church, they may, in the words of Erroll Hulse, be viewed as 'the enquirers and seekers after truth who attend the churches'.[1]

What does this young woman have to say to her companions? She tells them of that special time in which her beloved brought her into his banqueting hall and she was so impressed with the magnificence and splendour of it all that she was almost overcome.

This young lady was completely unaccustomed to finery. She knew a good deal about tents, vineyards, sunburn, foxes and apple trees, but virtually nothing about the king's banqueting hall. There the king entertained the best-known figures of the world. It was a place of exquisite finery and majesty, a place where the daintiest foods were served and where the king himself would appear in dazzling array.

The young Shulamite would probably have considered it honour enough for someone of her background to be allowed to see such a place. But the king was not content merely to give her a tour of the hall. He actually entertained her there! He took this common, ordinary girl to his banqueting hall and treated her as though she were some great world figure, as though she were royalty herself.

There was no doubt in this young woman's mind as to how it all came about. It was all explained in a single banner hanging over the table: 'Love'. Evidently, the kings of those days adorned their banqueting halls with banners, embroidered with various insignia which proclaimed the might and courage of the king. When the Shulamite entered the banqueting hall she noticed there was only one banner, and it declared, not the king's might and glory, but rather his love for her. She was there because the king loved her and desired to entertain her there. She was to enjoy these rich blessings solely because the king had set his love upon her.

There are distinct parallels between the Shulamite's experience in Solomon's banqueting hall and the Christian's experience of fellowship with Christ. In the first place, what the Shulamite found in Solomon's banqueting hall pictures what Christians find in their walk with Christ.

The abundance of life in Christ

As we reflect on God's abundant provision for his children, upon what Paul calls 'the riches of his grace' (Eph. 1:7), we realize several things about it.

It was pictured beforehand

Two Old Testament passages present powerful and compelling pictures of the believer feasting spiritually in the midst of
abundance. In the 23rd Psalm, David writes of the Lord as a
host who lavishly provides a table laden with food, perfumed
oil for anointing and a cup that overflows. Again, Isaiah speaks
of a bountiful feast in these terms:

> And in this mountain
> The LORD of hosts will make for all people
> A feast of choice pieces,
> A feast of wines on the lees,
> Of fat things full of marrow
> Of well-refined wines on the lees…
> He will swallow up death for ever
> And the Lord GOD will wipe away tears from all faces
> (Isa. 25:6-8).

The prophet Jeremiah strikes this same chord with the
words: 'I will satiate the soul of the priests with abundance,
and my people shall be satisfied with my goodness, says the
LORD' (Jer. 31:14).

Are we entitled to regard the Lord Jesus Christ as the fulfilment of these passages? Yes. The Lord Jesus himself seized
the imagery of Psalm 23 and applied it to himself when he
called himself the Good Shepherd. We also know it is legiti-
mate to link Isaiah's song of praise with Christ because two
apostles, Paul and John, do just this. Paul takes up the phrase
in Isaiah 25:8 about death being swallowed up and links it to
the resurrection of Christ (1 Cor. 15:54). And John draws from
that same verse to affirm that God will wipe away all tears
from the faces of his people when the eternal day dawns (Rev.
21:4). That day of rejoicing is made possible only through the
atoning death of Christ.

While the prophecy of Jeremiah refers first to Judah's return from captivity in Babylon, it is not exhausted by that event. Matthew Henry observes, 'All this is applicable to the spiritual blessings which the redeemed of the Lord enjoy by Jesus Christ, infinitely more valuable than corn, and wine, and oil, and the satisfaction of the soul which they have in the enjoyment of them.'[2]

It was specifically claimed by Christ

The Lord Jesus was keenly aware of the abundance pictured by David, Isaiah and Jeremiah, and had no hesitation in asserting that he had come for the express purpose of providing that abundance. Immediately before he identifies himself as the Good Shepherd, the Lord declares that he had come that his people should not only have life but have it 'more abundantly' (John 10:10). He seems to have had in mind the latter portion of Psalm 23, which describes the abundant provision of the Shepherd for the sheep.

If we go back to the beginning of Jesus' public ministry, we find him at a marriage feast in Cana. The governor of the feast had a thorny dilemma. The wine ran out before the feast was over. Jesus, knowing that wine was a symbol of joy, life and vitality, and thus a fitting emblem for the salvation he came to provide, seized the opportunity. He commanded that six waterpots be filled with water and that some be drawn out and taken to the governor. Somewhere along the line that water became the choicest wine. The fact that these waterpots were filled to the brim indicated something of the abundant nature of the salvation he had come to provide.

It is experienced by the Christian in salvation

The abundant life that Jesus came to provide actually becomes the precious possession of the sinner when he repents of his sin and casts himself totally upon the atoning death of Christ Jesus. At that point, he experiences a reception similar to that described in the parable of the prodigal son. That son, having thrown himself recklessly into riotous living and having reaped the whirlwind of misery and woe, finally made his way back to his father. As he went, he carefully rehearsed his speech. If his father would take him back, he would will-ingly become a hired servant. But his father had different ideas! Seeing him while he was still a good distance away, the father ran to his son, fell on his neck, and kissed him. He commanded that a robe be put around his shoulders, a ring on his finger and sandals on his feet. He ordered that the fatted calf should be killed and a merry celebration should take place (Luke 15:11-24).

The following lines capture the joy and satisfaction the sin-ner feels when he, like the prodigal, turns from his sin and comes to the Father:

All my life long I had panted
For a draught from some clear spring,
That I hoped would quench the burning
Of the thirst I felt within.

Feeding on the husks around me,
Till my strength was almost gone,
Longed my soul for something better,
Only still to hunger on.

Poor I was, and sought for riches,
Something that would satisfy,
But the dust I gathered round me
Only mocked my soul's sad cry.

Well of water, ever springing,
Bread of life so rich and free,

Untold wealth that never faileth,
My Redeemer is to me.

Hallelujah! I have found him
Whom my soul so long has craved!
Jesus satisfies my longings,
Through his blood I now am saved.

                                                (T. Williams)

The heavenly Father has a feast spread for each and every
one of those who come to him in faith. What a bountiful feast
it is! Open your Bible and begin to read. This whole book is
about God graciously restoring sinful men and women to fellowship with him through the person and work of the Lord
Jesus Christ. As you read, you will find insights into this stunning work of redemption. As you turn these insights over in
your mind, you will feel you are tasting rare delicacies. And
when you think you have exhausted all possible insights into
this glorious redemption, you will be amazed to find fresh supplies being carried in from the kitchen!

It is experienced by the Christian in discipleship

In addition to the insights Scripture gives us into the glories of
redemption, there are precious promises to sustain us. These
promises tell us of his care and presence through this life and
of the inheritance laid up for us in the life to come. The truths
and promises with which the Scriptures teem are rare delicacies to the child of God. No believer should be able to read the
Word of God for long before he finds himself at a veritable
banquet of soul-satisfying truths concerning Christ! But to do
so he must look for Christ 'in all the Scriptures'.

Along these lines, George Burrowes says, 'There is literally such a thing as feeding on truth; and the place where these

spiritual provisions are enjoyed in abundance may well be called the banqueting house. How superior to everything else in the world is the banquet spread for us by Jesus! The truths and doctrines of Scripture, so rich, better than thousands of gold and silver, are the means, sacred vessels brought from heaven, for conveying to us the food of the Spirit. Here we banquet on the riches of redeeming love. The man who feeds on fame, flattery, riches, power, has nothing better than the husks of the dying prodigal; while those who are Christ's share the luxuries of the marriage supper of the Lamb.'[3]

Experienced by the Christian in public worship

Another aspect of the Christian's feeding on the abundance of Christ is public worship. Matthew Henry says of the Shulamite entering Solomon's banqueting house, 'Surely then we may apply it to Christian assemblies, where the gospel is preached and gospel-ordinances are administered.'[4] Henry is not over-reaching here. David was fond of speaking of public worship in terms of experiencing abundance. He writes of God's people: 'They are abundantly satisfied with the fulness of your house, and you give them drink from the river of your pleasures' (Ps. 36:8).

He also tells us what he himself expected from public worship:

So I have looked for you in the sanctuary,
To see your power and your glory...
My soul shall be satisfied as with marrow and fatness,
And my mouth shall praise you with joyful lips
(Ps. 63:2,5).

Still further he writes, 'We shall be satisfied with the goodness of your house, of your holy temple' (Ps. 65:4).

In what exactly does this experience of blessing consist? Sadly, public worship has become for many dull and devoid of life. But whenever God's people gather to truly magnify their Lord, to dwell upon his glorious attributes, to worship in Spirit and in truth, to hear the preaching of Christ and his gospel of glory, to bow down before him in worship, love and praise — then they fully partake of the riches of his table, the wonders of his name. The abundance God's house offers to us ought to cause fervent love for the church to well up within us.

Experienced by the Christian in eternity

While the Lord provides bountifully and lavishly for his people in this world, this cannot compare with the bounty he promises in heaven. Here we dine at a table in the wilderness (Ps. 78:19), but in heaven there awaits us an unspeakably splendid and glorious event, the marriage supper of the Lamb (Rev. 19:7-9). Stuart Olyott writes, 'That final marriage supper will be a day of majesty and glory. It will be marked by the Groom rejoicing over his bride, by longings satisfied, by unbroken communion, by perfect expressions of love and by uncontainable joy.'[5]

The wedding customs of scriptural times required the bride and her attendants to gather at her home to prepare for the wedding, while the groom and his attendants prepared at his home. When the groom was ready, he would make his way to the bride's house. She, in the meanwhile, would be looking out of the window in eager anticipation of his coming. When he did arrive, he and his attendants would escort the bride back to his house for a gala wedding feast that would last for several days.

The Lord Jesus Christ has gone away to prepare to take his bride to himself (John 14:1-3). In turn, his bride, the church, is also preparing for that day. She waits on earth (1 Thess. 1:9-10), eagerly looking for him to return (Titus 2:13). The Lord Jesus for whom she waits will finally come again and escort her to his home (1 Thess. 4:13-18). Then that greatest of all feasts, the marriage supper of the Lamb, will take place with abounding joy and gladness.

> When he comes, our glorious King,
> All his ransomed home to bring,
> Then anew this song we'll sing
> Hallelujah! What a Saviour!
>
> (Philip P. Bliss)

The gracious nature of Christ's abundance

Secondly, there is a parallel between the way in which the Shulamite came to enjoy the abundance of Solomon's banqueting house and the way the Christian comes to enjoy the abundance of Christ. A sense of wonder and awe pervades the Shulamite's words in this Song. It was incredible to her that Solomon, King of Israel, arrayed in majesty and splendour, should love her.

She expresses this wonder early and often. It is there when she pleads with Solomon not to look upon her unfavourably because of the darkness of her sun-tanned skin (1:5-6). It is there when she relates her visit to the garden to see if the walnuts were ripening and the vines budding. These were the ordinary tasks of an ordinary day. But suddenly and dramatically everything changed. She puts it in these words:

> Before I was even aware,
> My soul had made me
> As the chariots of my noble people
>
> (6:12).

What happened to her while she was engaged in these mundane tasks? Evidently, it was at this point that she met

Solomon, and before she knew it she was whisked away, either metaphorically or literally, in one of his chariots. She was lifted from peasant girl to queen in a very sudden and unexpected manner. How amazing! We find that same sense of awe when she says, 'He brought me to the banqueting house' (2:4). An ordinary country girl in the king's imposing banqueting hall — what an astounding thing!

Those who enjoy fellowship with the Lord Jesus Christ can see themselves in this picture of the wide-eyed Shulamite standing in the splendour of the banqueting hall. We know we are in the banqueting hall of fellowship with the King of kings and Lord of lords only because he has set his love upon unlovely sinners such as us.

We were no more deserving of that love than was the young Shulamite. There was nothing about us to commend us to the Lord, nothing that should cause him to take an interest in us. The Lord did not bring us into fellowship with himself because there was something we could contribute to his wealth. What could a poor country girl contribute to King Solomon? Nothing! And what could we contribute to the Lord of glory? Nothing! We are in fellowship with him, then, simply because he has set his love upon us. The apostle Paul puts it in these words: 'But God demonstrates his own love toward us, in that while we were still sinners, Christ died for us' (Rom. 5:8).

In another place, Paul writes, 'For you know the grace of our Lord Jesus Christ, that though he was rich, yet for your sakes he became poor, that you through his poverty might become rich' (2 Cor. 8:9). The apostle John adds these words: 'In this is love, not that we loved God, but that he loved us and sent his Son *to be* the propitiation for our sins... We love him because he first loved us' (1 John 4:10,19).

Matthew Henry shares with us something of what is involved in God's gracious 'bringing us in'. He says it means that Christ 'wrought in me an inclination to draw nigh to God, helped me over my discouragements, took me by the hand, guided and led me, and gave me an *access* with boldness to God as a Father'.[6] Henry adds, 'We should never have come into the banqueting-house, never have been acquainted with spiritual pleasures, if Christ had not brought us, by opening for us a new and living way and opening in us a new and living fountain.'[7]

How did he do this? It was through love. Henry says, 'He brought me in with a banner displayed over my head, not as one he triumphed over, but as one he triumphed in.'[8] As we read Henry's thoughts on this matter, we marvel, as John Newton did, at the thought of God's amazing grace:

Amazing grace! (How sweet the sound!)
That saved a wretch like me!
I once was lost but now am found;
Was blind, but now I see.

'Twas grace that taught my heart to fear,
And grace my fears relieved.
How precious did that grace appear,
The hour I first believed!

If we are to function as children of God should, we must continually see the wonder of our salvation. And if we are to see the wonder of salvation, we must dwell upon the wide gap between what we were when the Lord found us and what, by God's free grace, we have become.

The Christian's response

The sense of being overwhelmed

Let's return to the Shulamite for a moment. Imagine her walking into this stately hall. The tables are laden with food.

Musicians are playing. Attendants stand ready to serve. Beautiful mosaics are all around. Fountains of water send out their silver spray. The fragrance of flowers fills the hall. The Bible tells us that Solomon's wealth and finery so overwhelmed the Queen of Sheba that there was 'no more spirit in her' (1 Kings 10:5). If this finery could have such an effect on another head of state, how would we expect the young Shulamite to respond, especially in the light of the fact that her presence there was due to Solomon's love for her?

She tells us what the effect was. She was overwhelmed by it. She says she was 'sick of love'. That means she was so overcome by it all that she felt faint. She had to take some food in order to overcome this faintness. 'Sustain me with cakes of raisins, refresh me with apples', she said (2:5). Many Christians have testified to having much the same experience as they reflected on the spiritual banquet spread before them by Christ.

Jonathan Edwards had such an experience: 'Once as I rode out into the woods for my health in 1737, having alighted from my horse in a retired place, as my manner commonly has been, to walk for divine contemplation and prayer, I had a view that for me was extraordinary, of the glory of the Son of God as Mediator between God and man, and his wonderful, great, full, pure and sweet grace and love, and meek and gentle condescension. This grace that appeared so calm and sweet appeared also great above the heavens. The Person of Christ appeared ineffably excellent, with an excellency great enough to swallow up all thought and conception, which continued, as near as I can judge, about an hour, which kept me the greater part of the time in a flood of tears and weeping aloud.'[9]

Edwards continued his account of this experience by saying, 'I felt an ardency of soul to be, what I know not otherwise how to express, emptied and annihilated; to lie in the dust and to be full of Christ alone; to love him with a holy and pure love; to trust in him; to live upon him; to serve and follow him and to be perfectly sanctified and made pure with a divine and heavenly purity.' [10]

Shutting out disruptions

The love and communion she enjoyed that night in the banqueting hall were still vivid in her mind as she described her experience to the daughters of Jerusalem. They were not just the experiences of a single feast. Her intense concern was to keep the experience of fellowship with the king flaming brightly. So as she recounts her experience in the banqueting hall to the daughters of Jerusalem, she registers her concern that nothing should be allowed to disrupt them. She likens this love relationship to the gazelles and does of the field — animals that are timorous by nature — and she urges her attendants to let the love she shared with her beloved run its course.

Those who have entered into some of the depths of fellowship and communion with Christ find themselves very concerned that nothing be allowed into their lives that would disrupt it. Comparing the Shulamite's visit to the banqueting hall with our experience of fellowship with Christ ought to give us pause for thought. We should recognize that there is far more to this business of walking in communion with the Lord Jesus Christ than most of us have ever realized. There are depths we have never experienced, heights we have never attained. May God help us to desire a greater experience of fellowship with our Lord and to begin to enter into it.

9.
The gracious voice of Christ

*'The voice of my beloved! Behold, he comes leaping upon
the mountains, skipping upon the hills ...'* (S. of S. 2:8-9).

These verses begin a section in which the voice of the beloved
is prominent. First there is what we may call the 'arresting
voice' that reaches the Shulamite while her beloved is still afar
off. The mere sound of his voice was sufficient to make her
exclaim, 'The voice of my beloved!' (2:8). Then follows what
the beloved said to the Shulamite when he had come near (2:10-
14). A little later we find the Shulamite describing her response
to her beloved's voice: 'My heart went out to him when he
spoke' (5:6). The emphasis in this section on the voice of the
beloved gives us the opportunity to contemplate the voice of
the Christian's beloved, the Lord Jesus Christ.

It goes without saying that the four Gospels have much to
say about the voice of Jesus — that is, about the words that he
spoke and the manner in which he spoke them. Very early in
Jesus' public ministry the citizens of his home town, Nazareth, 'marvelled at the gracious words which proceeded out
of his mouth' (Luke 4:22). A little later in Capernaum the
people were 'astonished at his teaching, for his Word was with
authority' (Luke 4:32). While he was there, Jesus cast a de-
mon out of a man, and the people were 'all amazed' and said
among themselves, 'What a word this is!' (Luke 4:33-36).

From these auspicious beginnings, the powerful, gracious
voice of Jesus continued to work. Jesus said, 'Rise up and

walk,' and lame men quit their beds. Jesus cried, 'Peace, be still,' and the rolling waves and boisterous wind immediately obeyed. Jesus called, 'Lazarus, come forth,' and a living Lazarus emerged from the tomb.

Jesus himself stressed the importance of his word. He likened it to good seed that fell on different kinds of soils, and urged his hearers to be fruitful in their response to it. He went further and likened those who heeded his word to a wise man who built his house on a rock, and those who refused to hear him to a foolish man who built on sand.

In John's Gospel, Jesus boldly asserts that he spoke only the words that the Father gave him to speak. God the Father testified to the importance and reliability of the words of Christ when he spoke from heaven to Peter, James and John: 'This is my beloved Son. Hear him' (Luke 9:35). This incident came hard on the heels of an episode in which Simon Peter had taken it upon himself to question the reliability of Jesus' word (Matt. 16:21-22).

In a better moment, Simon Peter himself testified to the glorious words of Christ. Many of Jesus' professing disciples, having just heard a pointed message on the necessity of his blood-atonement, turned away from him saying, 'This is a hard saying; who can understand it?' (John 6:60,66). Jesus responded, not by pleading with them to stay, but by putting this question squarely before his original twelve disciples: 'Do you also want to go away?' (John 6:67). Simon Peter, who so often stumbled and failed, rose to the occasion. 'Lord, to whom shall we go? You have the words of eternal life,' was his memorable response (John 6:68). The voice of Jesus was so compelling that officers who were sent to arrest him came back empty-handed saying, 'No man ever spoke like this man!' (John 7:45-46).

The apostle John heard the voice of Jesus in a different setting. Christ was now ascended to the right hand of the Father, and he appeared to John and spoke with a voice so awesome and majestic that John records that it was 'as the sound of many waters' (Rev. 1:15).

The voice of Jesus, so admirable and so marvellous, has spoken. And he continues to speak in our own day, to each and every child of God.

An awakening voice

When I read how the Shulamite heard her beloved's voice from afar and how, like a fleet gazelle, he crossed the mountains to come to her, I find myself thinking of how Christ came to his elect in their darkness and their need. There we were, to quote Charles Wesley, 'fast bound in sin and nature's night'. Or to use the apostle's even more graphic imagery, we were 'dead in trespasses and sins' (Eph. 2:1).

We lay in a spiritual graveyard, devoid of life and unable to do anything to help ourselves (dead men do not raise themselves from the dead). All was utterly bleak and completely hopeless. Then, as it were, we heard a penetrating, awakening voice, the voice of Christ Jesus saying, 'Arise, dead soul, I give you life.' Our spiritual eyelids fluttered and we began to stir. Jesus himself speaks of this spiritual resurrection in John's Gospel: 'Most assuredly, I say to you, he who hears my word and believes in him who sent me has everlasting life, and shall not come into judgement, but has passed from death into life. Most assuredly, I say to you, the hour is coming, and now is, when the dead will hear the voice of the Son of God; and those who hear will live' (John 5:24-25).

The dead of whom Jesus was speaking here are the same as those to whom Paul was referring in Ephesians 2:1 — those who are spiritually dead in their trespasses and sins. Jesus speaks later about the resurrection of the physical body (John

5:28-29). His subject here is the resurrection of the soul from spiritual death. And he emphasizes that it is only his voice that can waken dead souls and grant them spiritual life. Such things are not accomplished by polished programmes, entertaining worship and clever preachers, but by the voice of Christ. That voice makes the difference between eternal life and eternal death.

How does that voice come to us? The voice of Christ comes to us through the Word of God. Spiritual quickening does not occur except through the gospel of the Scriptures. As Paul emphatically affirms, 'Faith comes by hearing, and hearing by the Word of God' (Rom. 10:17). This truth moved William R. Newell to write:

> Years I spent in vanity and pride,
> Caring not my Lord was crucified,
> Knowing not it was for me he died
> On Calvary.
>
> By God's Word at last my sin I learned;
> Then I trembled at the law I'd spurned,
> Till my guilty soul imploring turned
> To Calvary.

I thank God for that awakening voice that came from afar, all the way from heaven itself. I thank God that the Lord Jesus Christ, my beloved, gladly surmounted every obstacle to come to me in my sin and make me his. He bounded over the mountain of my rebellion, over the mountain of my deadness and over the mountain of the curse of God's law; he did so that he might find me, along with all who now call him their beloved.

> Love found a way to redeem my soul,
> Love found a way that could make me whole;

Love sent my Lord to the cross of shame,
Love found a way, Oh, praise his holy name!

(Constance B. Reid).

Because of that bounding love that spoke peace to my heart,
I can take upon my own lips the Shulamite's words: 'My beloved is mine, and I am his' (v. 16).

An inviting voice

The voice that once awakened the spiritual ears of every believer did not then cease. It continues to sound as Christ invites his people to commune with him. Lovers always desire to commune with each other. It is one of love's most delightful joys. Solomon certainly desired to commune with the Shulamite. We find him saying to her:

Rise up, my love, my fair one,
And come away.
For lo, the winter is past,
The rain is over and gone.
The flowers appear on the earth;
The time of singing has come,
And the voice of the turtledove
Is heard in our land.
The fig tree puts forth her green figs,
And the vines with the tender grapes
Give a good smell.
Rise up, my love, my fair one,
And come away!

(2:10-13).

Solomon goes further to tell the Shulamite why he desired her to rise and go with him:

Let me see your countenance,
Let me hear your voice;
For your voice is sweet,
And your countenance is lovely

(2:14).

Solomon received immense delight from hearing the voice of the one he loved. He later says:

You who dwell in the gardens,
The companions listen for your voice —
Let me hear it!

(8:13).

As Solomon desired to hear the voice of the Shulamite, so Christ desires to hear the voice of his people. He calls us to communion with him. He longs to meet us 'in the secret places' (2:14) where he can hear us voice our prayer, our needs, our supplications and our praise. The proper response to the voice of Christ is the sound of our own voices. Perhaps the one thing Christ most wants to hear from his people is prayer for the work of his Spirit. We might say he is especially pleased when the church takes upon her lips the plea of the Shulamite:

Blow upon my garden,
That its spices may flow out.
Let my beloved come to his garden
And eat its pleasant fruits

(4:16).

Before the church can properly pray this prayer she must, however, heed the voice of her beloved by rising up and coming away. Are we to rise up? Yes. All too often our Lord finds us settled in complacency and apathy. And that complacency is completely out of keeping with what he has done for us.

'Come away' is a two-sided term. On one hand, it means to leave behind the territory we presently occupy and, on the other hand, to begin to occupy new territory. In other words, we are not only to come away *from* something, we are to come *to* something.

From what are we to come away? What does the Lord want us to leave behind? Perhaps he is calling us from 'the worship of this vain world's golden store'; perhaps he wants us to come away from a vacillating, superficial commitment. Or perhaps he is calling some to leave behind them festering resentment and hurt feelings. To yet another he appeals for a departure from shortness of temper and a sharpness of tongue. Perhaps he calls us to come away from petty and trifling concerns. J. M. Neale says we are to come away, 'further and further from everything that is opposed to him, that is not stamped with his image ... from every little thing that keeps you in the least from him'.[1]

Our Lord does more, however, than call to us to enjoy communion with himself. He gives us a powerful incentive for doing so — namely, what he has already done for us. And what has he done? To use the imagery Solomon employs with the Shulamite, he has brought spiritual springtime into our hearts and lives. Because of Christ Christians can apply the bridegroom's words in verses 12-13 to their own experience.

'The winter is past' (2:11). Winter is the time of deadness and barrenness, and those who know Christ will be quick to say there was a time when they lived in a spiritual winter. They were, as we have seen, spiritually dead. But through the grace of God they were granted spiritual life. The imagery of the passing of winter and the coming of spring is an appropriate way to convey the dramatic transformation that takes place when a person comes to know Christ.

'The rain is over and gone' (2:11). Rain suggests thunder-clouds, which are a fitting symbol of the wrath of God. The apostle John says, 'He who believes in the Son has everlasting life; and he who does not believe the Son shall not see life, but the wrath of God abides on him' (John 3:36). What a picture! The rebel sinner lives beneath the thunderclouds of God's judgement, but for the believer those storm clouds have vanished in the sunshine of God's grace.

'The time of singing has come' (2:12). To the Christian, the whole world takes on a brighter, happier appearance because of the peace and joy he has found in Christ, and he is able to sing, with George Wade Robinson:

> Heaven above is softer blue,
> Earth around is sweeter green;
> Something lives in every hue,
> Christless eyes have never seen;
> Birds with gladder songs o'erflow,
> Flowers with deeper beauties shine,
> Since I know as now I know,
> I am his, and he is mine.

'The voice of the turtledove is heard' (2:12). To the believer the dove can represent only one thing, namely, the Holy Spirit. When the Holy Spirit descended at Jesus' baptism, he came in the form of a dove. To say the Christian hears the voice of the dove is to say he hears the voice of the Holy Spirit. How does he hear this voice? Audibly? No. The Christian hears the voice of the Spirit in the Word of God. The Spirit does his work through that Word, as Paul confirmed when he called the Word of God 'the sword of the Spirit' (Eph. 6:17).

'The fig tree puts forth ... green figs and the vines ... give a good smell' (2:13). Here we have fruitfulness and fragrance combined, a combination that exists in the lives of God's children. Christians do not all bear the same amount of fruit, but every one bears fruit to some degree. When the fig tree bears green figs it is evidence that summer is near, the time when fruitfulness is fully realized. The believer may not bear, at the beginning of his Christian walk, the fruit he yields later in life. But there is evidence from the beginning that fruitfulness is coming, and this fruit is pleasing to God and man alike, just as 'The tender grapes give a good smell' (2:13).

The spiritual springtime enjoyed by the Christian is reason enough for him to respond to Christ's call to communion. How could he not desire to commune with one who has done so much for him?

A heeded voice

We have looked at the awakening voice of Christ that calls us from sin and makes us his own, a voice that now calls us to communion with him. Now we can go yet further. The voice that called us from afar, and brought us spiritual life, is still speaking. It is the voice of our Shepherd. As that voice sounds, we find that we are quite unable to shut it out or ignore it.

The Lord Jesus speaks of this reality in terms of a shepherd and his sheep. Sheep have a certain characteristic — they know the voice of their shepherd. Jesus says, 'And when he brings out his own sheep, he goes before them; and the sheep follow him, for they know his voice. Yet they will by no means follow a stranger, but will flee from him, for they do not know the voice of strangers' (John 10:4-5). He then proceeds to say, 'My sheep hear my voice, and I know them, and they follow me' (John 10:27). As we read these things, we surely find ourselves nodding in agreement. Yes, it is true, those who are the Lord's sheep both follow and obey the voice of their great Shepherd. All true sheep do! The one who says he is a sheep but has no desire to follow the Shepherd is confused about his identity. He is no sheep at all, but will at last be found among the goats.

Perhaps someone is saying, 'Just how do you, who consider yourselves sheep, hear the voice of your Shepherd?' We answer by pointing to the Bible, the written Word of God. It is there that we 'hear' the voice of Christ, and find the Shepherd's guidance. The psalmist says to the Lord, 'Your word is a lamp to my feet and a light to my path' (Ps. 119:105).

Have you ever considered what a blessing it is to have guidance in a dark, confused world such as this? Some people spend great sums each year seeking guidance and counsel, but the guidance they receive from man is flawed and feeble. But God graciously gives guidance to his people in his Word, and that guidance is always sure and true.

As I look into the Word of God, I also find strength and encouragement. Life has a way of grinding us down. As we seek to cope with all that it throws at us, we can easily become despondent and depressed. But the Word of God comforts us. It tells us of a heavenly Father who has loved us with an eternal, undying love, a love that he manifested in the supreme act of giving his only Son to die on a cross, that we might be saved from eternal destruction. It assures us that the Father who has gone to such an incredible length to save us will never let us go (Rom. 8:31-39), but will continue his work in us until he finally presents us faultless before the throne of his glory. As I read my Bible, I find accounts of God's wondrous works, and I find myself assured that his wisdom and power are unlimited and his grace is sufficient.

This leads me to the precious and glorious promises I find in Scripture. What promises they are! I have already referred to several: his promise to guide us, his promise to complete his work, his promise to bring us into heavenly glory, his promise to supply us with sufficient strength. And these are just a few of the promises that adorn the pages of Scripture. He has given us promises regarding prayer. He has given us promises regarding the Holy Spirit. He has given us promises regarding the church. He has given us promises regarding revival.

As I open this book and find Christ speaking to me through his instructions, his comfort, his past works and his ongoing promises, I realize anew why God puts such a premium upon his Word, even to the point where the psalmist writes, 'For you have magnified your word above all your name' (Ps. 138:2). Should we not join him in saying, 'Therefore I love your commandments more than gold, yes, than fine gold'? (Ps. 119:127).

As I read the Word of God I agree with the poet:

Though the cover is worn
And the pages are torn,
And though places bear traces of tears,
Yet more precious than gold
Is the Book, worn and old,
That can shatter and scatter my fears.

When I prayerfully look
In the precious old Book,
Many pleasures and treasures I see;
Many tokens of love
From the Father above,
Who is nearest and dearest to me.

This old Book is my guide,
'Tis a friend by my side,
It will lighten and brighten my way;

And each promise I find
Soothes and gladdens my mind
As I read it and heed it today.

(Author unknown)

Part of the Shulamite's long description of her beloved is
devoted to his lips: 'His lips are lilies, dripping liquid myrrh'
(5:13). The lilies to which she refers were of a brilliant red
colour. Myrrh was a resin used as a perfume. By putting these
two things together, the Shulamite was declaring that every
word that fell from her beloved's lips was as pleasant as the
sweetest perfume.

As we contemplate the instructions, the encouragements
and the promises of the precious Word of God, we may very
well adopt the Shulamite's imagery and liken the words of
Christ to the most pleasant perfume. Psalm 45 is a prophetic
preview of the Messiah and his bride, the church. Part of it is
taken up with the bride's musings as she waits for her groom
to appear and escort her to the marriage feast (vv. 2-9). The
very first thought that comes to her mind as she thinks about
him is related in these words:

You are fairer than the sons of men,
Grace is poured upon your lips;
Therefore God has blessed you for ever

(Ps. 45:2).

The church waits for her Saviour to appear (1 Thess.
1:9-10). There is much for her to muse about as she waits, and
one of those things is his Word. As she waits, she reads, and as
she reads she marvels, and says to her Lord, 'Grace is poured
upon your lips.' Do we understand this? To the extent that we
heed the Scripture, to that extent we hear the voice of Christ.

The resurrecting voice

The voice of Christ that has roused his people from their spiritual death and called them to life has more awakening to do. That same voice will one day sound in glorious triumph, as Jesus returns to this benighted earth, revealing himself as 'King of kings and Lord of lords' (Rev. 19:16). The dead will rise at the sounding of that voice, for he had this to say about that stunning moment: 'Do not marvel at this; for the hour is coming in which all who are in the graves will hear his voice and come forth — those who have done good, to the resurrection of life, and those who have done evil, to the resurrection of condemnation' (John 5:28-29).

There are, then, two resurrections for the believer. The first took place when the Lord Jesus raised him from spiritual death and granted him eternal life. The second is the resurrection of his body from the grave. For the unbeliever, however, there is only one resurrection — that solemn moment when he is raised to stand before God's judgement throne to give account of himself and to hear pronounced the sentence of eternal wrath. It is no wonder that the apostle John, as he surveyed that coming day, wrote, 'Blessed and holy is he who has part in the first resurrection. Over such the second death has no power' (Rev. 20:6).

We either have, as believers, two resurrections, the first spiritual and the second physical, separated by one death (physical); or else, as unbelievers, one resurrection (physical) and two deaths (physical and eternal). The believer is indeed 'blessed'. He is the happiest of men because he has received the greatest of all God's blessings, spiritual and eternal life, and has nothing to fear on the Day of Judgement.

10.
Declension: Christ's voice spurned

'I opened for my beloved, but my beloved had turned away and was gone...' (S. of S. 5:6).

The emphasis on the voice of the beloved continues in Song of Solomon 5:2-8, but there is a significant change. While the bride gladly heard and heeded her beloved's voice in chapter 2, here she spurns and rebuffs it.

Her beloved comes to her at night, knocks on the door, and speaks: 'Open for me, my sister, my love, my dove, my perfect one...' (5:2). We expect, of course, to read that the bride immediately goes to the door, and lets him in. But that is not what happens. Instead she lingers in bed and offers only a trivial excuse. She says she would have to get up out of a warm bed, put her robe on and get her feet dirty! What terrible inconvenience that would have caused! Clearly, there is some basic problem here from which we may learn. Let us, therefore, explore this matter further.

The beloved's appeal and the bride's response

The beloved comes to the door and speaks. Three characteristics of his appeal are immediately noticeable. It is direct, tender and urgent, and each of these features can be related to the voice of Christ speaking to his people.

The beloved knocks and says, 'Open for me.' The appeal was *so simple and straightforward* that she could not plead ignorance or misunderstanding. The gravity of her action is revealed here. She refused to honour his specific, simple request.

Then notice the *tenderness* of his appeal. He employs several terms of endearment to move her to do as he requested. He calls her 'my sister, my love, my dove, my perfect one', all of which are designed to evoke a warm response. Matthew Henry says, 'He not only gives her no hard names, nor upbraids her with unkindness in not sitting up for him, but, on the contrary, studies how to express his tender affection to her still.'[1]

Finally, his appeal was *urgent*. The beloved says, 'My head is covered with dew, my locks with the drops of the night.' There he stands, damp and chilly with the dew, while she is warm and comfortable in her self-indulgence. We might at first be inclined to chuckle at the situation. It is, after all, quite ludicrous. Her beloved is standing outside in the cold, knocking for entrance, and she refuses to be put to any trouble. At first it might have all seemed harmless to the bride herself, but she soon realized the seriousness of it.

Evidently there was a little opening beside the door latch, and the husband made a movement with his hand, as if to unlatch the door. But instead he suddenly withdrew his hand. Spurgeon says, 'In the Eastern door there is generally a place near the lock into which a man can put his hand, and there is a pin inside which, if removed, unfastens the door. Each one of these locks is different from another, so that no one usually understands how to open the door except the master.'[2]

The sight of her husband's hand somehow stirred the bride and she realized belatedly how lazy and thoughtless she had been in refusing to open the door. Even so, instead of going directly to the door, she took time to put on her perfume, which was the customary way of welcoming one's beloved. By the time she finally opened the door, however, he was gone. So the chastened bride began to search for her husband. Her search seemed fruitless for a time, and sad words are spoken: 'I sought him, but I could not find him; I called him, but he gave me no answer' (5:6).

The search proved to be very difficult. The watchmen of the city misinterpreted her reason for wandering about the city, and treated her very roughly (5:7).

Christ's voice and our response

This incident, of course, creates a poignant and challenging picture for the child of God. It warns him of a tragic possibility, that of spurning the voice of his Saviour and Lord. How does this fit with what we noted in the previous chapter — namely, that the Christian heeds the voice of Christ? Surely it is a contradiction to declare that the Christian heeds the voice of Christ and then to say that he can also spurn the voice of Christ? Sadly, the contradiction is sometimes a reality. The contradiction can be understood when we learn to distinguish between what is *normally* true of the believer and what is *occasionally* the case. Normally the Christian heeds the voice of Christ. That is the general tenor of a believer's life. But there are times when sin prevails and he spurns that voice.

Examples of this sad fact abound in Scripture. Simon Peter hears the Lord speak about his impending death at the hands of the chief priests and scribes and, without a moment's reflection, takes Jesus aside to put him right. 'Far be it from you, Lord', he protests. 'This shall not happen to you!' (Matt. 16:22). How urgently Peter needed the stern reminder that sounded from heaven on the Mount of Transfiguration: 'This is my beloved Son, in whom I am well pleased. Hear him!'

(Matt. 17:5). It was Simon again who heard the voice of Jesus warn his disciples to watch and pray (Matt. 26:40-41). Yet he failed to heed that word and went on to deny his Master three times.

So strong is this tendency to stop listening to the voice of Christ that the apostles frequently found it necessary to sound an alarm against it. Paul wrote to the Corinthians, 'If anyone thinks himself to be a prophet or spiritual, let him acknowledge that the things which I write to you are the commandments of the Lord' (1 Cor. 14:37). The author of Hebrews urged his readers to 'give the more earnest heed' to the things which they had heard (Heb. 2:1). He then proceeded to caution them about their dullness in hearing the word (Heb. 5:11). Again, towards the close of his epistle, he added this word of admonition: 'See that you do not refuse him who speaks. For if they did not escape who refused him who spoke on earth, much more shall we not escape if we turn away from him who speaks from heaven' (Heb. 12:25). James warned his readers to 'receive with meekness the implanted word' and cautions them to be doers of the word and not hearers only (James 1:21-25).

Perhaps the most gripping of all scriptures on this matter comes from the pen of the apostle John as he records letters from the risen, glorified Christ to the seven churches of Asia. Pointedly, Christ says to each church, 'He who has an ear, let him hear what the Spirit says to the churches...' (Rev. 2:7,11,17,29; 3:6,13,22). In the last of these letters, addressed to the smug, self-satisfied church of Laodicea, the Lord picks up the imagery of the Song of Solomon and pictures himself as standing outside the door of his own church, knocking for entry: 'Behold, I stand at the door and knock. If anyone hears my voice and opens the door, I will come in to him and dine with him, and he with me' (Rev. 3:20). As we read those measured, powerful words we cannot help but hear in them the same direct, tender and urgent tone used by the beloved in the Song of Solomon.

It is *a direct and clear appeal*. Christ calls upon his church to 'open the door' so that she might enjoy communion with him. There is nothing complicated or mysterious here. Her failure to open the door stems, not from confusion about the appeal, but purely from laziness, the desire not to be inconvenienced.

It is *a tender appeal*. Christ always seeks to move his church to action by speaking kindly and lovingly. He is never abrasive and cruel. Oh, that this picture would sink into our hearts! Christ knocks gently when he could break down the door, and speaks tenderly when he could berate us for our indolence.

It is also *an urgent appeal*. This is not because he is in any need, nor because there is any lack or deficiency in Christ that his church can supply. The urgency stems from his fervent desire to commune with his people. We should be ashamed that God's desire to fellowship with us is often greater than ours to commune with him.

The picture we have in the Song of Solomon is, therefore, strikingly real. The child of God, and even whole churches, can spurn the voice of Christ in the same way that the bride spurned the voice of her beloved. Let us always seek to be like those commended by God in Isaiah. 66:2:

> On this one will I look [with favour]:
> On him who is poor and of a contrite spirit,
> And who trembles at my word.

The terrible cost of spurning the voice of Christ

The bride paid a high price, in terms of anguish and suffering, for rebuffing her beloved. So too do Christians, and the church corporately, if they spurn the voice of Christ and do not heed his word. That cost can be summarized in one word — separation. Refusing to heed the voice of Christ causes him to hide himself from us.

True believers can never be separated from Christ in the sense that our union with him is severed or destroyed. The apostle Paul makes this clear with his triumphant question: 'Who shall separate us from the love of Christ?' (Rom. 8:35). But while we can never truly be separated from Christ, we may temporarily experience separation in terms of our communion with him. This is a common theme in Scripture. Several verses speak of the Lord hiding his face from his people. To Hosea's generation the Lord pronounced these solemn words:

> I will return again to my place
> Till they acknowledge their offence.
> Then they will seek my face;
> In their affliction they will diligently seek me
>
> (Hosea 5:15).

The people of Isaiah's time were to experience separation from God to the extent that they would ultimately cry,

> Look down from heaven,
> And see from your habitation, holy and glorious.
> Where are your zeal and your strength,
> The yearning of your heart and your mercies toward
>   me?
> Are they restrained?
>
> (Isa. 63:15).

A little later we find these people's sad admission to God: 'For you have hidden your face from us' (Isa. 64:7).

So believers, personally and corporately, may suffer the loss of God's felt presence. An arid dryness saps their spiritual joy and reduces their worship to a formality. Prayer meetings are devoid of life and preaching becomes a chore to both preacher and hearers alike. This is a common condition in our day.

The end of separation from Christ

How, then, can we gain a renewed sense of Christ? The account of the Shulamite and her beloved provides us with some guidance on this matter.

Seeking

When the Shulamite realized her beloved had withdrawn from her, she immediately began to seek him. Her search soon caught the attention of the watchmen of the city. Suspicious of her prowling about at that time of night, they struck and wounded her (5:7), but she remained undeterred. Her fervent seeking reminds us of that large body of Scripture that holds before us the need to seek the Lord.

For instance, the author of 1 Chronicles records David's words on this matter: 'Seek the LORD and his strength; seek his face evermore!' (1 Chron. 16:11). Later the same author records David's message to the leaders of Israel: 'Now set your heart and your soul to seek the LORD your God' (1 Chron. 22:19). In his psalms, David continually expressed the desire to seek the Lord, likening the intensity of his search to physical thirst (Ps. 42:1-2; 63:1).

Seeking the Lord is especially vital when we have driven him from us by our sin and indolence in spiritual matters. If we humble ourselves, pray, seek God's face and turn from our wicked ways, we can be assured that he will hear, forgive and heal (2 Chron. 7:14).

Do we wonder why we are seeing so little of the power and glory of God in our midst today? The answer is all too obvious. We have grieved the Lord by our apathy, and we have not felt the enormity of our loss. Only when we see that will we be driven to seek our Lord urgently, fervently and wholeheartedly. And only that kind of seeking will heal our relationship with him. Such seeking is extremely rare these days, so much so that those who engage in it may be misunderstood, as was the Shulamite by the watchmen. May God help us to consider that a small price to pay for the joy of true spiritual restoration.

Enlisting the help of others

After receiving abuse from the watchmen of the city, the Shulamite turned to the daughters of Jerusalem to enlist their help:

> I charge you...
> If you find my beloved,
> That you tell him I am lovesick!
>
> (5:8).

C. H. Spurgeon sees in her plea a picture of the child of God going to his fellow saints. We never need their help more than when we are in a cold and backslidden condition. Spurgeon offers this counsel to those who are in that sad state: 'Enlist your brother saints to pray for you. Go with them to their gatherings for prayer. Their company will not satisfy you without Jesus, but their company may help you find Jesus. Follow the footsteps of the flock, and you may by and by discover the Shepherd.'[3]

The twin tasks of seeking and enlisting ought to convince us that it is not an easy business to heal the breach when we have slighted Christ. Some think they can drive Christ away by their sin and easily bring him back. But if it were that easy, we would not duly prize the restoration of his experienced presence, and would soon drive him away again. Let me repeat that I am not talking about a Christian losing his salvation, but rather about losing the sense of Christ's presence and the comforts of knowing Christ. And these things, I say, are not easily restored. All who have backslidden know it to be so. Sometimes, indeed, we despair and wonder whether Christ will ever seem near again. Sometimes, as we pursue our search more vigorously, we find others do not understand but only treat us roughly. Even ministers of the gospel may fail to appreciate what we are going through. At such times we are truly cast upon the Lord.

Gracious visitation from the Lord

There is, thank God, another dimension to this matter of healing the breach between ourselves and our Lord — namely that it does not all depend on us. The Lord supplies us with his grace here, as he does at every other point in our lives. We can see the truth of our Lord's renewing grace by going back to chapter 2 of the Song. There we find the Shulamite saying the beloved had been like a gazelle to her (2:8-9).

What was behind this statement? The very matter we are concerned with — separation. Evidently, after a period of wonderful closeness in which they delighted in each other's company, the Shulamite had been separated for a time from her beloved. What caused this separation? The Shulamite mentions mountains and hills. Life presents us with many difficulties and challenges that so preoccupy us that our communion with Christ may be affected.

Sometimes a sense of separation from Christ is a means by which he furthers his purpose for our lives. The soul has its seasons, as does nature, and each season has a purpose. The

cold barrenness of winter makes possible the vitality, fruitfulness and fragrance of spring. In like manner, the Lord sometimes takes his people through barren times so that we might
come to be more fragrant and fruitful for him. He withdraws
from us so that we might feel how utterly helpless we are
without him, that we might not take for granted the privilege
of communion with him, but prize and treasure it.

But the mountains and the hills could not stop the beloved
from coming to the Shulamite. She caught a glimpse of him
gazing at her through the window. It was only a glimpse, but
that was enough to fill her heart with sheer delight.

As she mused on this visit, the bride realized how much
like a gazelle her beloved had been in bringing their separation
to an end. The gazelle is a very speedy animal with magnifi-
cent leaping ability. Her beloved, in gazelle-like fashion, had
come to her as quickly as possible and had leaped over formidable obstacles to do so.

Our mountains of difficulty and hills of care may make him
seem far away, but they are nothing to him. Like the gazelle,
he can easily and speedily leap over them to come to us.

We never know when the Lord is going to leap the barriers
and overwhelm us by a conscious experience of his presence
and grace. When we are out of communion with Christ we go
sighing along the way. We know we need to draw close to
him, but we do not seem to be able to do it. Sometimes we
almost despair as we wonder if we shall ever feel close to the
Lord again. Then suddenly we catch a glimpse of him. Maybe
it happens in a worship service. We are simply singing along
with the congregation, feeling dead and empty as we do so,
and one line from the hymn suddenly reaches out and touches
us with the presence of Christ. Or perhaps we catch a sight of
him as we hear the Scriptures expounded in a sermon, or as
we read the Bible ourselves. It may be that we suddenly be-

come aware of his closeness in a conversation with a friend, or as the people of God come together at the Lord's Supper.

However it happens, we are made to realize again the glories of redemption, and the icy coldness of our hearts begins to thaw. These warm, renewing glimpses of Christ pave the way for sweet communion to be restored, and the Christian finds himself nodding in agreement as he hears those familiar lines:

Sometimes a light surprises
The Christian as he sings;
It is the Lord who rises
With healing in his wings.

(William Cowper)

Thank God for such times of renewing visitation! We know, of course, that we are living in a land of shadows, and that we shall never be able to enjoy perfect communion with Christ until 'the day breaks and the shadows flee away'. But when such times occur, we find ourselves earnestly desiring that we might never be separated from Christ again.

We also know that the best we can hope for in this life of shadows is that the Lord Jesus will often come to spend time with us in our conscious experience. How often the shadow of separation from Christ falls across our paths! Thank God, a day is coming when the shadows will flee. Then there will be no more separation from him. Communion with him will be perfect and permanent. We now see through a glass darkly, but then we shall see face to face (1 Cor. 13:12). No more will we have to content ourselves with glimpses of our Lord. But until that day comes, we have to pray constantly that the Lord will sustain us with frequent visits in which our consciousness of communion with him is strengthened and renewed.

11.
The friendship of Christ

'This is my beloved, and this is my friend' (S. of S. 5:16).

The daughters of Jerusalem asked the Shulamite why her beloved was so special to her (5:9). She proceeded to answer detail by detail until she had gone from his head to his feet. She brings her description to a conclusion with these words:

> Yes, he is altogether lovely.
> This is my beloved,
> And this is my friend,
> O daughters of Jerusalem!
>
> (5:16).

It may seem to us as if the Shulamite is descending from a very high plane to one that is considerably lower when she concludes by describing her 'beloved' as her 'friend'. To our way of thinking, love is much higher than friendship. Surely, if the Shulamite had wanted to end her description on a truly high note, she would simply have said, 'This is my beloved.'

Friendship in our day is a very wide term that covers anything from a casual acquaintance to an extremely loyal relationship. Unfortunately, it often seems that there are more of the former than the latter. When the Bible talks about friendship, however, it usually has in mind a loyal relationship. Friendship in the Bible is the firm comradeship or partnership that springs from the highest love. This is borne out by these words from Solomon himself: 'A friend loves at all times' (Prov. 17:17).

The love of a friend is so deep and true that he or she is willing to tell us the truth even when it hurts. Solomon stated this fact when he wrote, 'Faithful are the wounds of a friend, but the kisses of an enemy are deceitful' (Prov. 27:6).

In calling her beloved her 'friend', the Shulamite was not, therefore, descending to a lower level at all, but rather reinforcing all that the term 'beloved' conveys. She was referring to intense love and unswerving loyalty.

As we worked our way through her description of her beloved, we found each detail to be admirably suited to the Lord Jesus Christ. It is the same with the terms she uses here. Christ is an altogether lovely friend to the Christian. When the believer thinks of the friendship of Christ, his mind gravitates to yet another of Solomon's proverbs: 'A man who has friends must himself be friendly, but there is a friend who sticks closer than a brother' (Prov. 18:24). As far as the Christian is concerned, there can be no doubt about the identity of the friend that 'sticks closer than a brother'. It is none other than the Lord Jesus.

The friendship of Jesus takes us to that moving and memorable night before Jesus was crucified. The scene was the upper room where Jesus had gathered with his disciples to observe the Passover. Supper was now ended. Judas Iscariot had gone out into the dark night of betrayal and spiritual ruin. Jesus was left alone with his eleven true disciples. To these men Jesus spoke explicitly about his impending death. They were crushed with sorrow and dismay.

Nothing stands out more clearly, on that night heavy with emotion, than the tenderness of the Lord Jesus Christ towards his sorrowing disciples. How tenderly he spoke about the Father's house (John 14:1-3), the privilege of prayer (John 14:12-14), the coming of the Holy Spirit (John 14:15-18; 16:5-

15), the gift of his peace (John 14:25-27) and the 'little while' they would be separated from him (John 16:16-22).

Tucked away in the middle of all those comforting words, we find that term 'friends'. It crops up twice in these words: 'Greater love has no one than this, than to lay down one's life for his friends. You are my friends if you do whatever I command you' (John 15:13-14). It appears again in the very next verse: 'No longer do I call you servants, for a servant does not know what his master is doing; but I have called you friends, for all things that I heard from my Father I have made known to you' (John 15:15).

One of the primary truths that emerges from Jesus' words on that night is that his friendship is different from any other. Out of all the special friendships most of us enjoy, none can compare with the friendship of the Lord Jesus Christ.

A different kind of friendship

It began in a different way

How is Christ's friendship different? We can say, first, that it begins in a different way from other friendships. We all know how friendships are usually formed. People are attracted to each other by mutual interests and become friends. In other words, most friendships come about as a result of the mutual choice of people who are equals.

But the friendship of Christ is different. It comes about as a result of his choosing us. And this happened, not while we were his equals (something we never have been and never will be), but rather when we were his enemies (Rom. 5:8-10). When Jesus called his disciples his 'friends', he stressed that it was because of his choice of them: 'You did not choose me, but I chose you...' (John 15:16).

What was true of those disciples is true of all Christians. The apostle Paul tells the believers in Ephesus that they were chosen in Christ 'before the foundation of the world' (Eph. 1:4). Other Scriptures stress that Christ determined to be our friend while we were still his enemies. The 'carnal mind', the mind we are all born with, is 'enmity against God' and 'not subject to the law of God' (Rom. 8:7). The truth of the matter is that those of who us enjoy the friendship of Jesus were not at first friendly to him at all. We were in a state of rebellion and hostility towards him. We were not even interested in his friendship. We were interested only in ourselves and in going our own way.

But, in spite of it all, the Lord Jesus Christ befriended us. He did so first in eternity by the election of grace, and then in time by the regenerating work of the Holy Spirit. In that regeneration, he replaced the stony heart of hostility with the soft heart of friendship.

> I've found a friend, Oh, such a friend!
> He loved me ere I knew him;
> He drew me with the cords of love,
> And thus he bound me to him;
> And round my heart still closely twine
> Those ties which naught can sever,
> For I am his, and he is mine,
> For ever and for ever.
>
> (James G. Small)

It was manifested in a different way

This brings us to another difference between mere human friendships and the friendship of Jesus — that is, the way it is manifested. Firstly, the friendship of Christ is *measured by the*

Father's love for the Son. Jesus' words to his disciples convey this great truth: 'As the Father loved me, I also have loved you' (John 15:9). His friendship for them flowed from a love that was like the Father's love towards him.

Imagine it: the Lord Jesus loves his friends in the same way the Father loves him. How does God the Father love Christ? We are totally out of our depth here. But we can say at the very least that the Father loves the Son with a love that is without measure, without change and without end. And Christ loves his friends in the same way — without measure (no line can fathom it), without change (he does not love us less one day than he does another) and without end (the love that is the same today as it was yesterday will always be the same). No wonder the biblical authors appear almost breathless as they contemplate that love. The apostle John must have felt this way when he exclaimed, 'Behold what manner of love the Father has bestowed on us, that we should be called children of God!' (1 John 3:1).

Secondly, Christ's friendship is *measured by the cross*. Such an indication of the degree of Jesus' friendship is found in John 15:13, where he speaks of laying down his life for them. We are all familiar with stories about people laying down their lives for their friends. A house is on fire, and a man dashes in to pull his friend to safety and perishes in the process. A soldier is wounded and the enemy is laying down a withering fusillade, but his friend rushes back to pull him to safety and is killed.

But we make a serious mistake if we think the death of Jesus for his friends was in the same category as such heroic acts. You see, when one man lays down his life for another he is doing an admirable thing, but he is only speeding up something that will inevitably happen anyway. We are all going to die sooner or later, and our dying for a friend only hastens the event. Jesus, on the other hand, did not have to die. When he took our humanity at Bethlehem and went to the cross on Golgotha, he was doing something he did not have to do.

Even that does not say it all. Jesus not only died a death he did not have to die, but he also died a death like no other death. It was far more than a physical phenomenon. It was a death in which he experienced an eternity of being forsaken by God in the place and stead of his friends!

> The love of God is greater far
> Than tongue or pen can ever tell;
> It goes beyond the highest star,
> And reaches to the lowest hell...
>
> Could we with ink the ocean fill,
> And were the skies of parchment made;
> Were every stalk on earth a quill,
> And every man a scribe by trade;
> To write the love of God above
> Would drain the ocean dry;
> Nor could the scroll contain the whole,
> Though stretched from sky to sky.
>
> (Frederick M. Lehman)

We shall never appreciate the love manifested in the death of Christ until we understand why it was necessary and what it accomplished. There Christ interposed himself between the wrath of God the Father and sinners, and absorbed that wrath himself. He took the sinner's place.

Some words from the Shulamite give us insight into the nature of Christ's death on the cross. She referred to her beloved as an apple tree in the forest (2:3). Among all the trees found there, he was unique, without peer or rival. She then proceeds to say, 'I sat down in his shade with great delight, and his fruit was sweet to my taste' (2:3).

Her reference to shade takes us to the very core of the cross of Christ. The burning rays of the sun were falling upon the Shulamite until she came under the apple tree. That tree came between her and the sun and she was shaded.

Now let the sun represent the wrath of God, and the Shulamite the sinner upon whom those rays are falling. The apple tree, of course, represents Christ and his atoning death. He absorbed the rays of God's wrath, and all those who flee to him find shade from that wrath. Charles Spurgeon puts it like this:

God's anger, like the hot noonday sun, falls on me; how can I escape it? There is no escape from the anger of God except by an interposer. What is a shadow? Is it not caused by the interposition of the bough or the rock, or whatever it may be, which comes between us and the sun? If we sit under a tree in the shadow, it is because the tree receives the heat, and so we escape from it. Jesus Christ's great office is the Interposer, the Mediator, the Substitute, the Atonement, the Sacrifice, and when we hide beneath him we are screened. God's wrath cannot come on us, because it has come upon him on our behalf.

When Christ my screen is interposed
Between the sun and me,
My joyful heart and lips unclosed,
Adore the glorious tree.[1]

As we reflect on the shade that Christ provides from the scorching heat of God's wrath, we see that he has fulfilled the prophecy of Isaiah:

Behold, a king will reign in righteousness,
And princes will rule with justice.

A man will be as a hiding place from the wind,
And a cover from the tempest,
As rivers of water in a dry place,
As the shadow of a great rock in a weary land
                                                (Isa. 32:1-2).

A different kind of life

Because the believer has in Christ a different kind of friend, a
friend like no other, his whole life is different.

Different priorities

For one thing, he has a wholly different set of priorities. As
Jesus spoke to his disciples about his friendship with them, he
pointed out that they could not simply live like others. His
friendship put certain demands upon them. They could not
play fast and loose with his commands. Part of being a friend
of Christ is doing what he asks: 'You are my friends if you do
whatever I command you' (John 15:14).

One of the commands of Jesus is that his followers should
love one another (John 15:17). We cannot claim to be his friends
if we do not love his other friends. Yet another priority that
flows from the friendship of Christ is being willing to endure
the hostility of the world. Jesus says, 'If you were of the world,
the world would love its own. Yet because you are not of the
world, but I chose you out of the world, therefore the world
hates you' (John 15:19). Some vainly imagine that it is possible to be both the friend of the world and the friend of Christ,
but the Bible assures us that it is not: 'Do you not know that
friendship with the world is enmity with God? Whoever therefore wants to be a friend of the world makes himself an enemy
of God' (James 4:4).

Divine comfort and peace

These priorities may make it seem that the Christian life is nothing but difficulty and hardship. It does entail these things, as Jesus made very clear. But it also brings peace and comfort that unbelievers do not know. Jesus pointed this out to his disciples in these precious words: 'Peace I leave with you, my peace I give to you; not as the world gives do I give to you. Let not your heart be troubled, neither let it be afraid' (John 14:27). The Christian has great peace from knowing Christ. In him he has one to whom he can bring his griefs and cares. The author of Hebrews urges his readers to 'come boldly to the throne of grace' so that they might 'obtain mercy and find grace to help in time of need' (Heb. 4:16).

> What a Friend we have in Jesus,
> All our sins and griefs to bear!
> What a privilege to carry
> Everything to God in prayer!
>
> (Joseph Scriven)

In Christ the believer has a friend to guide him (Ps. 73:24; Prov. 3:5-6), help him (Ps. 33:20; 40:17; Heb. 13:6), keep him (Ps. 121:5; Jude 24), sustain him (Ps. 55:22), sympathize with him (Heb. 4:15) and provide for his needs (Phil. 4:19). In addition to these things, the believer has peace because he knows he has in Christ a friend who will never leave him or forsake him. He can join the psalmist in saying, 'When my father and my mother forsake me, then the LORD will take care of me' (Ps. 27:10).

The author of Hebrews writes of Christ, 'He himself has said, "I will never leave you nor forsake you" ' (Heb. 13:5). That not only applies to each and every day of life, it also applies to the hour of death. What an hour that is! Other friends are unable to help us then. They are helpless, but our divine friend is not helpless. He is there in the gathering gloom to meet us and escort us safely home. Every believer can take David's words as his own:

> Yea, though I walk through the valley of the shadow of
>   death,
> I will fear no evil;
> For you are with me;
> Your rod and your staff, they comfort me
>
> (Ps. 23:4).

After this life is over comes the judgement. Oh, how we shall need a friend on that solemn day! Earthly friends will be of no value but the Christian has the friend he needs. The Lord Jesus who befriended him in this life will be there with him. It is not so with the wicked. Edward D. Griffin powerfully describes that coming day and sounds a word of warning to those who do not know Christ: 'Then, when all your sins shall be displayed before assembled worlds, and the curse fastened to each shall be ready to fall upon your defenceless head, and nothing to arrest the rushing war but the mediatorial shield, and your earthly friends unable to help either you or themselves; then will you in the fullest sense, though alas too late, feel your need of that friend which sticketh closer than a brother. You would then give ten thousand worlds for that interest in him which you now refuse.'[2]

As the child of God tabulates all that is involved in the friendship of Jesus, he cannot help but join J. Wilbur Chapman in singing:

> Jesus! What a friend for sinners!
> Jesus! Lover of my soul;
> Friends may fail me, foes assail me,
> He, my Saviour, makes me whole.

Jesus! what a help in sorrow!
While the billows o'er me roll,
Even when my heart is breaking,
He, my comfort, helps my soul.

Jesus! what a guide and keeper!
While the tempest still is high,
Storms about me, night o'ertakes me,
He, my pilot, hears my cry.

Hallelujah! what a Saviour!
Hallelujah! what a friend!
Saving, helping, keeping, loving,
He is with me to the end.

Section III

The exaltation of the church

12.
A church made fair

'Behold, you are fair, my love! Behold, you are fair!...'
(S. of S. 1:15; see also 4:1,7; 6:10; 7:6).

The common denominator in the above verses is the word
'fair'. It is a word that signifies perfect beauty. As we study
these verses, it will become apparent, firstly, that the bride's
beauty was so overwhelming that it could only be adequately
portrayed by a rich variety of figures and, secondly, that she
was *completely* beautiful. There was no flaw to be found any-
where in her person.

Almost all beauty is flawed, but that was not the case with
this bride. Her eyes were as gentle and tender as the eyes of a
dove (1:15; 4:1). Her hair was as black and shining as the
goats grazing on Mt Gilead (4:1). Her teeth glistened with the
whiteness of newly shorn sheep, the upper and lower teeth
perfectly matched like twins, while her lips, like a thread of
scarlet, needed no make-up to beautify them (4:3). All of which
made her mouth most lovely. Her temples (or perhaps cheeks)
were red, the colour of a freshly sliced pomegranate (4:3).
Her neck was straight and stately like the tower of David, a
tower built to store the shields of a thousand mighty men (4:4).
The breasts of the young woman were as beautiful and appealing as fawns feeding among the lilies (4:5).

Another detailed description of the Shulamite is found in
Song of Solomon 7:1-11. There the beloved calls attention to
her feet (7:1), thighs (7:1), navel (7:2), waist (7:2) breasts

(7:3,7-8), neck (7:4), eyes (7:4), nose (7:4), head (7:5), hair (7:5) and stature (7:7). In addition to all these things, her breath was pleasant (7:8) and, in the words of Stuart Olyott, her mouth was 'as exhilarating to him as wine is to the faint'.[1]

All of these qualities made such a profound impression on Solomon that he was compelled to exclaim repeatedly: 'Behold, you are fair, my love! Behold, you are fair!' (1:15; 4:1). He also declares: 'You are all fair, my love, and there is no spot in you' (4:7). He even goes so far as to say:

> You have ravished my heart,
> My sister, my spouse;
> You have ravished my heart
> With one look of your eyes,
> With one link of your necklace.
> How fair is your love,
> My sister, my spouse!
>
>   (4:9-10).

He goes yet further in his praise for her with these words:

> Who is she who looks forth as the morning,
> Fair as the moon,
> Clear as the sun,
> Awesome as an army with banners?
>
>   (6:10).

The beloved's praise reaches a climax in these words: 'How fair and how pleasant you are, O love, with your delights!' (7:6). These descriptions and exclamations make it clear that Solomon was quite overwhelmed with the beauty of his bride. This comes as no surprise to us. We are familiar with such expressions from someone who is smitten with love.

But how many of us think of Christ and his love for his church in these terms? How many of us think of him as being smitten with the beauty of the church? How many of us think of Christ as exclaiming, 'How fair!' when he speaks of his heavenly bride? How many of us would choose the word 'overwhelmed' to describe the effect his people have on Christ?

I dare say that most of us have a very different picture in mind. We are painfully aware of the deficiencies of the church. If asked to describe how Christ thinks of her, we might suggest that he should be dejected and disappointed. Certainly he cannot possibly be thrilled with his church, can he? Our tendency is perhaps to think of Christ as being saddled with a church that falls far short of his hopes and expectations.

But it is not so! Although the church is far from perfect in this world, there is still much about her that is fair, and the Lord delights in her fairness even now. We know he does because we have explicit affirmations in Scripture to that effect. The psalmist writes, 'For the LORD takes pleasure in his people; he will beautify the humble with salvation' (Ps. 149:4). And the prophet Isaiah adds, 'And as the bridegroom rejoices over the bride, so shall your God rejoice over you' (Isa. 62:5). Another prophet, Zephaniah, pictures the Lord singing with delight over his people:

The LORD your God in your midst,
The Mighty One, will save;
He will rejoice over you with gladness,
He will quiet you in his love,
He will rejoice over you with singing
(Zeph. 3:17).

Let us try to understand how it is that Christ can view his church with such enthusiasm.

The vile material from which the church is made

It is difficult for those who make up the church to think of her as being fair to Christ for one simple reason: we know what we were before we became part of the church. We know the apostle Paul was right when he said, 'We all once conducted ourselves in the lusts of our flesh, fulfilling the desires of the flesh and of the mind, and were by nature children of wrath, just as the others' (Eph. 2:3). We have to nod in agreement when Paul describes those who are separate from Christ as 'having their understanding darkened, being alienated from the life of God, because of the ignorance that is in them, because of the hardening of their heart' (Eph. 4:18).

The truth of the matter is this: those of us who now make up the church were anything but fair by nature. We were sinners, under the wrath of God. There was nothing in us to commend us to God. Occasionally someone will explain God's reason for saving his people by saying, 'Even though we were sinners, God saw some good in us.' Nothing could be further from the truth. Such a statement contradicts Paul's piercing indictment of the human race:

> There is none righteous, no, not one;
> There is none who understands;
> There is none who seeks after God.
> They have all gone out of the way;
> They have together become unprofitable;
> There is none who does good, no, not one
> (Rom. 3:10-12).

Paul's words leave no room for misunderstanding. God does not find any good in us, for no part of our human nature has escaped the dreadful blight of sin. No Christian will quibble with Paul's analysis. We all became aware of the plague of our hearts when the Lord in grace convicted us of our sinful state and brought us to himself.

We can think of a lot of words to describe the material from which the Lord Jesus constructs his church, but 'fair' is not one of them. We might use words such as 'foul', or 'vile', or 'polluted', but certainly not 'fair'. How, in the light of the nature of those who constitute the church, can anyone suggest that the Lord Jesus sees his church as 'fair'?

We are not what we were

The answer to that question is that those who make up the church are not what they once were. In other words, the Lord Jesus Christ did not just take us as we were and put us into his church. He has changed us. Nowhere is that change more forcefully and clearly stated than in these words from the apostle Paul: 'Therefore, if anyone is in Christ, he is a new creation; old things have passed away; behold, all things have become new' (2 Cor. 5:17).

How Paul delighted to remind his fellow-believers of this transformation! He loved to paint in contrasting colours what they had been and what they had become. A powerful example of this is found in his first letter to the Corinthians. Paul writes, 'Do you not know that the unrighteous will not inherit the kingdom of God? Do not be deceived. Neither fornicators, nor idolaters, nor adulterers, nor homosexuals, nor sodomites, nor thieves, nor covetous, nor drunkards, nor revilers, nor extortioners will inherit the kingdom of God. And such were some of you. But you were washed, but you were sanctified, but you were justified in the name of the Lord Jesus and by the Spirit of our God' (1 Cor. 6:9-11).

The same great contrast is present in these words the apostle wrote to Titus: 'For we ourselves were also once foolish, disobedient, deceived, serving various lusts and pleasures, living in malice and envy, hateful and hating one another. But when the kindness and the love of God our Saviour toward man appeared, not by works of righteousness which we have done, but according to his mercy he saved us, through the washing of regeneration and renewing of the Holy Spirit, whom he poured out on us abundantly through Jesus Christ our Saviour, that having been justified by his grace we should become heirs according to the hope of eternal life' (Titus 3:3-7).

In his letter to the Ephesians, Paul says, 'Husbands, love your wives, just as Christ also loved the church and gave himself for it, that he might sanctify and cleanse it with the washing of water by the word, that he might present it to himself a glorious church, not having spot or wrinkle or any such thing, but that it should be holy and without blemish' (Eph. 5:25-27).

The church is fair to Christ, then, because he has made her fair! All who belong to her have been washed and made fair. Certain words jump out at us from these verses, words that convey the nature of this washing that has made us fair in the sight of God.

Regeneration

The first thing that happens in those who are washed by Christ is spiritual regeneration. Paul writes, 'Not by works of righteousness which we have done, but according to his mercy he saved us, through the washing of regeneration and renewing of the Holy Spirit' (Titus 3:5). The sinner is dead in his sins and dead towards God. He does not have the mind to comprehend the truth of God, the will to embrace the demands of God, or the heart to love God. If we were to wait for the sinner to move towards God, we should wait for ever. The sinner has no more disposition or inclination to do so than a mouse has to approach a cat.

This word 'regeneration' tells us that God moves towards the sinner. He comes, as it were, to the spiritual cemetery, finds the sinner there, and grants him life. God does not stand at the graveside and plead with the dead sinner to come out of his grave, but rather imparts life to the dead. The sinner has no ability to leave his grave. He cannot even hear the message, let alone respond to it.

No, God does not pin his plan of salvation on the sinner bringing himself out of spiritual deadness. God first grants the sinner life and then, and only then, can the sinner hear God speak and respond to his speaking.

Regeneration, then, is that gracious act in which God, by his Holy Spirit, intervenes in the life of the sinner and not only enables him to trust in Christ as his Saviour, but also grants him a whole new disposition — that is, one to love Christ and serve him. It is God's gracious granting of spiritual life to spiritually dead sinners.

It is interesting that the apostle Paul relates this act of regeneration to 'washing' (Titus 3:5). How is it possible to equate God's gift of spiritual life to sinners with washing? The answer is that at the same time as God imparts spiritual life to the sinner, he also cleanses him from his sin, from his love for sin, from his hostility towards God and from his inability to understand, love and serve God.

The cleansing agent

We must not leave this matter of the washing of regeneration without noting the 'water' that God uses to bring it about. Paul identifies it for us, saying that Christ gave himself for the church 'that he might sanctify and cleanse it with the washing of water by the word' (Eph. 5:25-26). James agrees, telling us that God 'brought us forth' — that is, imparted spiritual life to us — 'by the word of truth' (James 1:18). The apostle Peter also says our spiritual life comes about 'through the word of God which lives and abides for ever' (1 Peter 1:23).

God does his regenerating work by his Spirit through his Word, the Holy Scriptures. Through that Word God makes the sinner aware that he must some day give an account to God, his Creator and rightful Sovereign; that God is holy himself and demands holiness of his creatures; and that he, the sinner, has no righteousness or merit to commend him to God, but rather is a guilty sinner. This word also makes it clear that this fateful accounting is hastening towards the sinner at a fearful speed. It is all most devastating.

Thank God, this same Word has incredibly glorious news to offer — namely, that the holy God before whom we must give account has provided a way for our sins to be forgiven and cleansed, through the redeeming death of his Son. It is all there in the precious Word of God, and by using that Word to make the sinner aware of these things, God grants him spiritual life.

Justification

A second aspect of what is involved in the church being made fair is justification. We might call this 'legal washing'. Justification takes us into a court of law. A guilty man stands before a judge to hear his sentence of condemnation pronounced. Instead he hears the judge say that he is not condemned but acquitted!

All who live in this world and breathe God's air are under his law. That law pronounces a curse. It says that if we break God's commandments we must endure his wrath and be separated from him in an eternal hell (2 Thess. 1:9). Every last one of us comes under the penalty of this law because we all break God's commandments in thought, in word and in deed (Rom. 3:10-18,23). It would seem that there is no hope for us. God's law stands over us demanding perfect obedience and declaring eternal judgement on all disobedience. We are the criminals in God's court of law and God himself is the judge.

Yet, thank God, the case is not hopeless. Instead of hearing God pronounce their condemnation, those who make up the church have heard him order their acquittal. In other words, they are 'justified' — that is, declared righteous, or just, before God.

How does this magnificently wonderful thing come about? It is certainly not by God's arbitrarily setting aside his law. God does not simply say to those whom he justifies, 'You have broken my law but even though it requires condemnation, I am going to ignore it and let you go free.' God cannot do that. He must honour his own law. If he refused to do so he would violate his own just and holy nature. Here is the glory of the gospel. God has, at one and the same time, found a way both to honour his law and to let guilty sinners go free. In other words, he found a way to be the 'just justifier' by satisfying the demands of his law and yet pronouncing guilty sinners guiltless.

That way is his own Son, the Lord Jesus Christ. Christ took our humanity upon himself, thus placing himself under the law of God. He lived in perfect obedience to that law and then went to the cross and endured the wrath of God on behalf of the chosen sinners who compose his church. He could endure the wrath of God for the sins of others because he had no sins of his own. Because he bore the wrath of God on behalf of his church there is no wrath left for them to endure. God's justice is satisfied, then, because its sentence has been carried out. Because Christ suffered the penalty for the sins of his people, and the penalty cannot be exacted twice, God commands those for whom Christ died to go free.

The church is fair to the triune God, therefore, because Christ himself took her sins and has cleansed her from her sin. But there is more to it than that. Paul declares that God 'made him who knew no sin to be sin for us, that we might become the righteousness of God in him' (2 Cor. 5:21). The church is not only clean in God's sight, but she has received the glorious dress of Christ's righteousness to replace the filthy rags of her sin. She is fair because she is endowed with the seamless robe of the righteousness of Christ. Each of her members can join W. Gadsby in saying:

> I'm blest, I'm blest, for ever blest;
> My rags are gone, and I am dressed
> In garments white as snow;
> I'm married to the Lord the Lamb,
> Whose beauties I can ne'er explain,
> Nor half his glory show.

Sanctification

The meaning of sanctification

There is a sense in which sanctification is already complete. There is another sense in which it is ongoing. The first sense may be referred to as positional sanctification and the latter as progressive.

Positional sanctification. The word 'sanctify' means 'to set apart'. It should be noted that the apostle Paul, in the verse cited above (1 Cor. 6:11), places sanctification between washing (regeneration) and justification. He writes, 'But you were washed, but you were sanctified, but you were justified in the name of the Lord Jesus and by the Spirit of our God.' It should also be noted that Paul uses the aorist tense in describing each of these stages of salvation. This signifies that the action is completed. In one sense, therefore, every believer in Christ is sanctified at the same time as he is washed and justified. From that moment onwards, he is set apart by God for the purpose of holy living.

Progressive sanctification. Scripture also speaks of sanctification as an ongoing work. Paul says Christ gave himself for the church, 'that he might sanctify and cleanse it with the washing of water by the word, that he might present it to himself a glorious church, not having spot or wrinkle or any such thing, but that it should be holy and without blemish' (Eph. 5:26-27). Making the church fair is a process. It begins with regeneration and justification and it ends, as we shall soon see, in glorification. The middle stage of the process, that stage that fills the gap between the initial cleansing (regeneration) and the ultimate cleansing (glorification), is 'progressive' sanctification. For the sake of brevity, I will just call it 'sanctification'.

Why is this middle stage necessary? The fact is that those who make up the church still have much sin in their lives even though they have been regenerated and justified, and sanctification deals with that sin. The fact that the church is regenerated and justified does not mean we are completely clean. In regeneration we are given a new disposition. In justification we are released from the condemnation of God's law. But there is still much sin to be rooted out of our lives. This rooting out takes place through the process of sanctification. Paul's words to the Ephesians make it clear that Christ died for the church with a view to this process of sanctification.

Martyn Lloyd-Jones writes on this matter of sin: 'The New Testament never stops at the guilt; it always goes on to this further idea of our being cleansed from the power of sin also. Indeed I want to add even to that. This cleansing is not only from the guilt of sin, and from the power of sin, it is also from the pollution of sin.'[2]

L. Berkhof defines sanctification as 'that gracious and continuous operation of the Holy Spirit, by which He delivers the justified sinner from the pollution of sin, renews his whole nature in the image of God, and enables him to perform good works'.[3]

It cannot be emphasized strongly enough that this is part of the Lord's cleansing of his church. It is something that he carries forward. This requires emphasis because so many split justification and sanctification. They insist that it is possible to receive one part of our Lord's saving work while rejecting another part. In other words, they say it is possible to receive forgiveness of sins by receiving Christ as Saviour while rejecting him as Lord. The so-called 'carnal Christian' is supposedly one who has done this. He has received forgiveness for his sins but, although he is now saved, he continues to live in sin. He has taken justification, but he refuses to take sanctification.

Paul throws all this out of the window by asserting that the Lord is cleansing his church, and sanctification is part of that process. We do not, therefore, sign up for sanctification. As soon as we are saved, we are automatically enrolled in the school of sanctification, and our Lord is the headmaster of that school.

In his letter to the Philippians, Paul says, 'He who has begun a good work in you will complete it until the day of Jesus Christ' (Phil. 1:6). The Lord does not begin the work of salvation when we believe in him as Saviour, and then stand helplessly by if we refuse to be sanctified. He carries the work forward — and he has a multitude of ways of doing so (including chastisement, Heb. 12:5-11).

The primary means of sanctification

The primary agent our Lord uses for carrying out his work of sanctification is laid out for us by Paul. He says the sanctification of the church takes place 'with the washing of water by the word' (Eph. 5:26). The truths of the Word of God are essential not only in the act of regeneration, but also in the process of sanctification. How does the Word of God sanctify us? For one thing, it reminds us that we have, as noted above, already been sanctified! It tells us that God has already set us apart for himself and that we are, therefore, to recognize who we are and to live accordingly.

In addition to this, Scripture also defines sin for us. It tells us what pleases God and what does not. It also holds before us truths that motivate us to break away from sin and live increasingly for God — namely, God's holiness and hatred of sin, his determination to judge sin and his willingness to forgive sin. The Bible also contributes to our sanctification by reminding us of the ministry of the Holy Spirit. We are not alone in our struggle against sin. The Holy Spirit indwells each Christian for the specific purpose of strengthening and helping him to combat sin and to live for God.

Furthermore, the Bible assures us of a day in which the Lord Jesus Christ will return to take his people from this world of sin. The promise of the glory of that day fills us with amazement and makes us *want* to live holy lives. The apostle John calls our attention to the wonder of what awaits us and the demand it places upon us: 'Beloved, now we are children of God; and it has not yet been revealed what we shall be, but we know that when he is revealed, we shall be like him, for we shall see him as he is. And everyone who has this hope in him purifies himself, just as he is pure' (1 John 3:2-3).

If he is going to do all this for us, we must certainly desire to please him.

The respects in which the church is fair to Christ

The Lord's work of regeneration, justification and sanctification means, as noted above, that there is already much about the church in which he delights. In what other respects can it be said that the church is fair to Christ at the present time? We do not have to speculate about this. Scripture affirms that the Lord delights in the church's worship and praise (Ps. 69:31; 87:2), her faith (Heb. 11:6), her prayers (Prov. 15:8), her holiness (1 Sam. 15:22), her reverence for him and her hope in him (Ps. 147:11), her ministry (Phil. 4:18) and, as we shall see, her graces.

The Song of Solomon calls our attention to additional aspects of the church that please Christ — namely, her correspondence, or likeness, to himself and her lack of correspondence to the world. The former is conveyed to us by these words: 'Like a lily among thorns, so is my love among the daughters' (2:2). The position of these words is very important. The beloved has just referred to himself as the rose of Sharon and the lily of the valleys. The very next thing he says is that his bride is also like a lily. He is a lily; she is a lily. There is a correspondence between the two.

One of the reasons why Christ has such a fervent love for the church is that there is a correspondence between him and his church. He loves the church because he sees himself in the church. How could it be any other way? Christ is perfect in every respect, and when he sees himself in his church, he cannot help but praise the church and love her.

We see this same correspondence in two phrases from the New Testament. On one occasion Jesus said, 'I am the light of the world' (John 8:12). In the Sermon on the Mount, he said to his disciples, 'You are the light of the world' (Matt. 5:14). His nature is reproduced in us. The apostle Paul tells us that the regenerating grace of Christ makes us new creatures who are made 'according to the image of him who created him' (Col. 3:10), while Peter says Christians are actually 'partakers of the divine nature' (2 Peter 1:4). Our conformity to Christ is far from perfect now, but we are 'predestined to be conformed to the image of his Son' (Rom. 8:29) and, when Christ finally appears, 'We shall be like him, for we shall see him as he is' (1 John 3:2).

The beloved is not content merely to refer to his bride as a lily. He proceeds to describe those around her. She was not just one lily among many lilies. Far from it! She was like a lily among thorns. The Lord Jesus says the same thing about his church. This tells us not only how he regards his people, but also how he regards those who are not part of his church. The church is as beautiful to him as a lily, but unbelievers are as thorns to him. Thorns are often used in Scripture as an emblem for the wicked. In his last words to the nation of Israel, David says:

> But the sons of rebellion shall all be as thorns thrust
> away,
> Because they cannot be taken with hands.
> But the man who touches them
> Must be armed with iron and the shaft of a spear,
> And they shall be utterly burned with fire in their place
> (2 Sam. 23:6-7).

The prophet Micah says of evil men, 'The best of them is like a brier; the most upright is sharper than a thorn hedge' (Micah 7:4).

Ezekiel's prophecy contains similar imagery (Ezek. 2:6), and in his parable of the sower, Jesus described one kind of hearer of the Word of God in terms of seed received among thorns (Matt. 13:7,22). What does this imagery tell us about unbelievers? They are unfruitful and unprofitable to God.

This is how Christians themselves once were — thorns! But what a transformation has taken place! Nothing could be greater than the difference between a lily and a thorn, and that is the difference between the church and the world — a difference that brings delight to Christ.

Glorification

The final aspect of Christ's work of making his church fair is
known as glorification. This takes us to that time when the
Lord Jesus will come again and take his bride from this world
to join him in the glories of heaven. At that point she will be
free from every vestige of sin and her beauty will be incapable
of improvement. She will be completely and perfectly fair.

The apostle Paul pointed the Ephesians to that day with
these words: 'Christ also loved the church and gave himself
for it, that he might sanctify and cleanse it with the washing of
water by the word, that he might present it to himself a glorious church, not having spot or wrinkle or any such thing, but
that it should be holy and without blemish' (Eph. 5:25-27).

Some contend that it is a mistake to regard the Song of
Solomon as a picture of Christ and the church. The apostle
Paul apparently did not think so. As he thought about the Lord
Jesus presenting his bride to himself, he seems to have deliberately chosen to echo Solomon's words: 'You are all fair, my
love, and there is no spot in you' (4:7). Some day the Lord's
process of making his church fair will be complete, and he will
look upon her and repeat to her those very words.

The apostle John was enabled to see that grand moment
when the work of redemption is finally complete and the spotless church is joined in marriage to her Lord. Speaking of the
church, he says, 'To her it was granted to be arrayed in fine
linen, clean and bright, for the fine linen is the righteous acts
of the saints' (Rev. 19:8).

The church is not without spot or blemish in this world.
She is in the process of sanctification. Some day that process
will be complete. Sanctification will give way to glorification
and the church will be spotless. It will all be a result of her
mighty Lord bringing it about. To him belongs the praise, as
Jude notes in the closing words of his epistle:

Now to him who is able to keep you from stumbling,
And to present you faultless
Before the presence of his glory with exceeding joy,
To God our Saviour,
Who alone is wise,
Be glory and majesty,
Dominion and power,
Both now and for ever.
Amen

(Jude 24-25).

13.
For Christ alone

'A garden enclosed is my sister, my spouse...'
(S. of S. 4:12 - 5:1).

Solomon obviously took enormous delight in the beauty of his bride, but he took even greater delight in knowing that this beautiful woman had reserved herself for him, and him alone. The images Solomon uses to describe her convey this delight. He refers to her here as 'a garden enclosed', as 'a spring shut up' and as 'a fountain sealed' (4:12). These are terms of exclusiveness. Solomon's bride did not give herself to anyone, but only to him. A walled garden is one that only the owner and the gardener can enter. The waters of a spring that has been 'shut up' and a fountain that has been 'sealed' are not available to all, but only to the one who has placed them out of bounds.

Solomon's delight that the bride reserves herself solely for him is also conveyed by the prominence of the pronoun 'my', appearing eleven times in the space of two verses (4:12; 5:1).

As Solomon rejoiced in the singleness of the Shulamite's heart, so Christ rejoices in the devotion of his people. The church belongs exclusively to Christ. Before the world began she was given to him by God the Father. We might say that it was then that the wall was built about the church. The purpose of putting a wall around a garden is to separate it from the surrounding area. By his electing love, the Father placed a wall around the church, separating it from the world, and gave it to his Son.

Christ has a garden walled around,
A paradise of fruitful ground,
Chosen by love and fenced by grace,
From out the world's wide wilderness.

(Isaac Watts)[1]

In receiving this gift from the Father, the Son also received an assignment. Those who were enclosed by electing love would have to be redeemed from the horrid ruin of sin. In the fulness of time, the Lord Jesus Christ came into this world for that express purpose. The apostle Paul says Christ 'gave himself for us, that he might redeem us from every lawless deed and purify for himself his own special people...' (Titus 2:14). Peter strikes much the same note in these words: 'But you are a chosen generation, a royal priesthood, a holy nation, his own special people, that you may proclaim the praises of him who called you out of darkness into his marvellous light; who once were not a people but are now the people of God, who had not obtained mercy but now have obtained mercy' (1 Peter 2:9-10).

Here is the purpose of the plan of redemption. Here is the reason why God the Father gave his Son a people, why Christ came to this world and died for them, why they are regenerated by the Holy Spirit. Here is the purpose for which they are justified and sanctified, and for which they will eventually be glorified. It is all to the end that the Son might have his own special people.

The church seeks to glorify Christ alone

The Bible gives us several dimensions to explore concerning the church as Christ's special people. One truth it lays before us is this: the church lives for Christ's glory alone.

It could be no other way. The church knows that she owes everything to Christ. By his death on the cross, he lifted her from the pit of sin and condemnation. The church can never forget this. The words of the apostle Paul echo in her mind: 'You were bought at a price; therefore glorify God in your body and in your spirit, which are God's' (1 Cor. 6:20). The church reflects on this and sings with Elvina M. Hall:

Jesus paid it all,
All to him I owe;
Sin had left a crimson stain,
He washed it white as snow.

Those who make up the church understand this. They understand that they are part of a plan that stretches from eternity to eternity. They know that this plan called for the Lord Jesus Christ to bear their sin and that through that act they have been freed for ever from condemnation and given title to glory. They realize that Christ has purchased them to be his special people. Because they know these things they are always glad to join Count Zinzendorf in saying, 'I have one passion; it is Christ and Christ alone.'[2]

The church proclaims Christ alone

Pluralism and tolerance are the watchwords of the day. All claims to truth are considered equally valid and, we are told, it is the height of arrogance to suggest that one claim to truth is in any way superior to others. Many do not hesitate to affirm that there is no such thing as absolute truth (failing to see as they do so that they are themselves stating an absolute!). What is the church to do in such a climate? Is she to be content to offer the gospel as one more item on the buffet of religious ideas? The church has no choice at all about this matter. She is under orders, even in a climate that is hostile to truth, to proclaim that Christ is the only way of salvation and that he, and he alone, is Lord of all.

He alone is Saviour

Why must the church proclaim Christ as the only hope for eternal salvation? The first reason for doing so is that the Lord Jesus himself unequivocally declared this truth. On the night before he was crucified, the Lord said to his disciples, 'I am the way, the truth, and the life. No one comes to the Father except through me' (John 14:6).

Another reason is that the apostles did so. When Peter and John were called before the authorities to explain how they had healed a lame man, Peter declared the uniqueness of Christ in these words: 'Nor is there salvation in any other, for there is no other name under heaven given among men by which we must be saved' (Acts 4:12).

He alone is Lord

In addition to proclaiming Jesus as Saviour, the church is bound to proclaim him as Lord of all. The very essence of Christianity is bound up in the affirmation: 'Jesus is Lord.' No one can be a Christian who does not heartily subscribe to this statement of faith (Rom. 10:9). What does it mean to say Jesus is Lord? It means we recognize him as the sovereign Ruler of all things and we submit to him as such.

How do we know Jesus is Lord? The Gospel accounts furnish us with evidence upon evidence. He commanded the winds and the waves, and they obeyed. He caused the blind to see, the deaf to hear, the lame to walk and the dead to live again. But the supreme evidence of his lordship is his own resurrection from the grave. Simon Peter hammered this truth home on the Day of Pentecost: 'This Jesus God has raised up... Therefore let all the house of Israel know assuredly that God has made this Jesus, whom you crucified, both Lord and Christ' (Acts 2:32,36).

Even with evidence for Christ's lordship on every hand, many deny it. But denying it does not change the reality. Jesus Christ is Lord whether we acknowledge him as such or not, and Scripture assures us that a day is coming when all without exception will be compelled to acknowledge it. The apostle Paul declares '... that at the name of Jesus every knee should bow, of those in heaven, and of those on earth, and of those under the earth, and that every tongue should confess that Jesus Christ is Lord, to the glory of God the Father' (Phil. 2:10-11).

The church worships Christ alone

Since the church readily acknowledges that Christ alone is Lord of all, it follows that she worships none but him, and the Father he reveals. In the wilderness, immediately after he was baptized, the Lord Jesus Christ was assaulted with three temptations from Satan. In the last of these temptations, Satan showed Jesus all the kingdoms of the world and promised to give them to him, if only he would fall down and worship him. The Lord responded by saying emphatically, 'Away with you, Satan! For it is written, "You shall worship the Lord your God, and him only you shall serve" ' (Matt. 4:10).

Today, as then, there are many false gods. We are tempted to worship 'the vain world's golden store', for covetousness, Paul tells us, is idolatry (Eph. 5:5). Some would have us bow at the shrines of nature, humanism or evolution, worshipping the creature rather than the Creator (Rom. 1:25). Yet others seem to point us to a Christian God, but when we approach we find that he is not the God and Father of our Lord Jesus

Christ, who reveals himself in Christ alone. Let us be clear. Only Jesus Christ reveals the true Father, for only he is 'the image of the invisible God' (Col. 1:15; see also Heb. 1:3).

The church depends on Christ alone for the present and the future

Another inevitable corollary of the lordship of Christ is that the church trusts him, and him alone. She trusts in his redeeming work for her eternal salvation and she continues to trust him as she lives in this world. She trusts him for the strength and grace to face her trials and difficulties here, and she trusts him to remove her eventually from this sphere and take her home to himself.

This matter of the church's trust in Christ is illustrated very well by Song of Solomon 8:5. Solomon and his bride are seen walking back towards the city after strolling together in a barren, wilderness area. Someone, perhaps a relative, takes note of them and exclaims: 'Who is this coming up from the wilderness, leaning upon her beloved?' The question does not signify doubt about the bride's identity, but rather a happy recognition of what has taken place. The Shulamite maiden is now the wife of the great King Solomon. Who would ever have thought such a thing could happen? The force of these words, then, is as follows: 'Can this really be the simple country maiden I know, who is walking with the king and in dependence on him?' The one who utters these words is filled with wonder over what he is seeing.

The speaker notices something in particular — namely, that the bride is leaning on her beloved. Here is the key for the church as she walks through the wilderness of this world. She must lean on her beloved, the Lord Jesus Christ. The word 'leaning' is rich in implications. It means the church is conscious of her own weakness. She realizes that this wilderness is too much for her, that she lacks the strength, in and of herself, to cope with it. But it also means she is keenly aware that her beloved does have the strength and the wisdom that living in the wilderness demands.

The scene pictured in this verse also tells us that the Lord Jesus Christ is near and can be leaned upon. There is a paradox here. In one sense, as we have noted, the Lord Jesus is absent from us. He is at the right hand of God making intercession for all who believe. But in another sense he is here with us — not physically, of course, but in the person of the Holy Spirit whom the Father sent to be our helper and to abide with us for ever (John 14:16-18). It was in this way that Jesus fulfilled his promise to be with us 'always' (Matt. 28:20). The Spirit of Christ dwelling in the believer and the church constitutes a real presence and, because the Lord Jesus is present in this way, we can indeed lean upon him.

Our verse also means that the Lord Jesus cares for us enough to let us lean on him. He sympathizes with us in this wilderness, as the author of Hebrews indicates: 'For we do not have a High Priest who cannot sympathize with our weaknesses, but was in all points tempted as we are, yet without sin. Let us therefore come boldly to the throne of grace, that we may obtain mercy and find grace to help in time of need' (Heb. 4:15-16). Whether as the church collectively, or as individual believers, we are not dependent on our own resources as we walk through this world, but rather on the resources of Christ, who is near and who cares deeply for his people. The church traverses this wilderness, then, with the words of Proverbs 3:5-6 ringing in her ears:

Trust in the LORD with all your heart,
And lean not on your own understanding;
In all your ways acknowledge him,
And he shall direct your paths.

Are you struggling hard, dear Christian, against the hardships of this world? Are you heartbroken and seemingly without strength to go on? Does life seem to be too much for you? The answer for you is this: lean on your beloved! Trust him in every circumstance of life. Trust him to care, to strengthen you, to have a purpose for you in the midst of your difficulties and finally to bring you out of the wilderness. Trust every promise he has given in his Word. Yes, lean on your beloved, singing:

Leaning, leaning, safe and secure from all alarms,
Leaning, leaning, leaning on the everlasting arms.
                                        (Elisha A. Hoffman)

The church bears fruit for Christ alone

We began this chapter by looking at Solomon's use of the imagery of a garden to express his delight in the fact that his bride belongs exclusively to him. This metaphor opens up yet another dimension of the church's devotion to Christ alone. The purpose of a garden is to bear fruit for the gardener. The Lord has the same purpose for his church. The apostle John records Jesus' words to his disciples only hours before he was crucified: 'By this my Father is glorified, that you bear much fruit; so you will be my disciples' (John 15:8). A little later he added, 'You did not choose me, but I chose you and appointed you that you should go and bear fruit, and that your fruit should remain' (John 15:16).

What kind of fruit does the Christian produce? In his letter to the Galatians, the apostle Paul gives a list of nine graces that comprise what he calls the fruit of the Spirit: 'love, joy, peace, long-suffering, kindness, goodness, faithfulness, gentleness, self-control' (Gal. 5:22-23).

Love is that disposition that compels us to give freely and sacrificially in the service of others. Love marks us out as the people of God. Jesus himself says, 'By this all will know that you are my disciples, if you have love for one another' (John 13:35).

Joy is that irrepressible happiness that bubbles up within us and manifests itself in our conduct even when circumstances are difficult and unpleasant. The Lord so worked this grace into Paul's life that he was able to write an epistle of joy from his prison cell. In that epistle he calls the Philippians to share his joy: 'Rejoice in the Lord always. Again I will say, rejoice!' (Phil. 4:4). In unfurling the banner of joy, Paul reveals its source — 'the Lord'. No matter how difficult the Christian's circumstances, he always has reason to rejoice because he always has the Lord.

Peace may be considered an offshoot of joy. It is that tranquillity of mind which enables us to keep our emotional equilibrium in even the most trying circumstances of life. It also has its source in God, being 'the peace of God, which surpasses all understanding, [and which] will guard your hearts and minds through Christ Jesus' (Phil. 4:7).

Long-suffering is that grace that enables us to put up with all that is unpleasant in others, and to do so with love and patience. It is an even temper which puts up with exasperating conduct in others without flying into a rage.

Kindness means the Christian has a benign heart and a soft answer, a serene, loving and sympathizing temper. It is the absence of harshness.

Goodness is the active expression of kindness. One way in which the beloved praised his bride, as we noted earlier, was by likening her to a dove. This speaks volumes about her gentle, harmless temperament. No one is afraid of a dove! And that dovelike quality is evident in the life of the Christian.

Faithfulness means that the one in whom the Spirit of God dwells is absolutely honest and utterly dependable in all his dealings. He is unswerving in his commitments.

Gentleness, or 'meekness', means that the Christian is sensitive and not self-assertive. As one who has been mastered by God, the believer is not concerned about himself and his rights.

Self-control is that grace that enables the Christian to keep his appetites, desires and passions under control.

We can go further and say that these godly attitudes find their expression in good works. Thus whenever the Christian does things out of a heart of love for Christ, and out of concern for the spiritual well-being of others, fruit is borne to the glory of God. The apostle Paul says, 'For we are his workmanship, created in Christ Jesus for good works, which God prepared beforehand that we should walk in them' (Eph. 2:10). Several other Scriptures also emphasize the importance of good works (1 Tim. 2:10; 6:18; 2 Tim. 3:17; Titus 2:7,14; 3:8; Heb. 10:24; 1 Peter 2:12).

The Lord has planted the church for the express purpose that she should bring forth fruit. And, note this well, the Lord receives immense pleasure and delight from his garden. He loves to look upon a life that he has reclaimed from the wilderness of sin and see it yield a rich variety of fruit.

My best Beloved keeps his throne
On hills of light, in worlds unknown;
But he descends and shows his face
In the young gardens of his grace.

In vineyards, planted by his hand
Where fruitful trees in order stand,
He feeds among the spicy beds,
Where lilies show their spotless heads.

(Isaac Watts)

14.
The church and the gospel

'A fountain of gardens, a well of living waters...'
'Awake O north wind, and come, O south! Blow upon my
garden, that its spices may flow out'
'How beautiful are your feet...' (S. of S. 4:15,16; 7:1).

The Song of Solomon contains two smaller 'songs' from Solomon. In each of these songs, Solomon praises his bride (4:1-15; 7:1-9) and each is followed by the bride's response (4:16; 7:10). The first response was evidently spoken immediately after the bridegroom's song of praise. The second is a little different. The beloved seems to have fallen asleep shortly after praising his bride (7:9) while she remains awake. As she contemplates his praise of her, she expresses her delight that she belongs to such a one and that he belongs to her (7:10). When he at last awakes she urges him to retreat with her to a place where they can enjoy their love without interruption or distraction (7:11-13).

Each aspect of the beloved's songs and the bride's responses can be applied in some way to Christ's relationship to his church, but three features seem to have special significance. I refer to the closing words of the first song (4:15), the response of the bride to this song (4:16) and the opening words of the second song (7:1).

I suggest these have special significance because they make reference to the church's task of proclaiming the gospel of Jesus Christ. The first of these special features, the fountain of waters, has to do with the nature of the gospel — that is, it is like refreshing water. The second, the blowing wind, has to do with the church's empowerment for the task, or her effectiveness in the task, of proclaiming the gospel. The final feature, the feet, has to do with the Lord's delight in his church's proclamation.

The nature of the gospel message

Solomon ends his first song of praise by calling his bride 'a fountain of gardens, a well of living waters' (4:15). These words may be applied to the Lord's view of his bride, the church, in the following way.

On one occasion the Lord encountered a Samaritan woman from the city of Sychar. She had come to Jacob's well outside the city to draw water. Jesus used this fact to drive home to her heart the truth about the spiritual life he had come to provide. He gestured towards the water in Jacob's well and said, 'Whoever drinks of this water will thirst again, but whoever drinks of the water that I shall give him will never thirst. But the water that I shall give him will become in him a fountain of water springing up into everlasting life' (John 4:13-14). The spiritual life Jesus was about to grant her is received by every believer. It enters into the individual soul and remains there as a constant source of satisfaction and refreshment in this life and it finally issues into eternal life. But that is not all.

John tells us about another occasion in which the Lord Jesus resorted to this fountain imagery. He had gone up to the Feast of Tabernacles in Jerusalem. This feast was the most elaborate of the seven the Jews observed each year. Its purpose was to re-enact their fathers' wilderness wanderings. To do this the people erected and occupied temporary booths during the feast. They also commemorated God's miraculous provision of water for their fathers in the wilderness. They did so by engaging in a dramatic water-pouring ceremony on each of the feast's seven days. Every day water was drawn in a golden pitcher from the pool of Siloam and carried in a grand procession to the temple where it was poured out on the altar. On the seventh day, 'that great day of the feast' (John 7:37), there were seven processions instead of one.

It was on this last day of the feast that Jesus suddenly cried out to the gathered crowd, 'If anyone thirsts, let him come to me and drink. He who believes in me, as the Scripture has said, out of his heart will flow rivers of living water' (John 7:37-38). When a person trusts Christ as his Lord and Saviour he not only finds his own spiritual thirst quenched, but he also becomes a means of quenching that thirst in others. William Hendriksen writes, 'The blessed one becomes, by God's sovereign grace, a channel of abundant blessings to others.'[1]

J. C. Ryle adds: 'That almost every believer, whose life is spared after he believes, becomes a fountain of blessing and good to others, is a simple matter of fact, which needs no illustration. A truly converted man always desires the conversion of others, and labours to promote it. Even the thief on the cross, short as his life was after he repented, cared for his brother thief; and from the words he spoke have flowed "rivers of living water" over this sinful world for more than eighteen hundred years. He alone has been a fountain of blessing.'[2] Ryle's words only need to be updated by a hundred years or so to still be true.

John offers an explanation of Jesus' words at the feast. He says they were spoken concerning the Holy Spirit whom those believing in Christ would receive. The Holy Spirit did not come in fulness upon believers until the Day of Pentecost, after Christ had returned to the Father. When he did come upon them, the words of Jesus were confirmed as those believers became zealous witnesses for Christ. All of this was a fulfilment of the prophecy we find in Isaiah:

… I will pour water on him who is thirsty
And floods on the dry ground;
I will pour my Spirit on your descendants,
And my blessing on your offspring;
They will spring up among the grass
Like willows by the watercourses

(Isa. 44:3-4).

The accounts in John's Gospel show us that believers not only have spiritual life springing up within them, but they also find it flowing out to others. In each of these instances Jesus spoke of individual believers, but his words apply to the church as a whole. The church is a composite of all believers. If each believer has a well of water springing up and flowing out, it is certainly valid to say the church also is a fountain of water. Indeed, we have New Testament confirmation that the words of Solomon to his bride may be taken as the words of Christ to his church. We are told in Ephesians 2:22 that the church is 'a habitation of God in the Spirit'. As the Holy Spirit indwells the believer, so he does also the church. Unless this were so, she would be powerless to serve her Lord.

The empowerment of the church for her task

In Solomon's first song of praise to his bride, he likens her to a beautiful garden (4:12-15). She immediately responds to his praise with these words:

Awake, O north wind,
And come, O south!
Blow upon my garden,
That its spices may flow out…

(4:16).

Her response might be paraphrased as follows: 'Am I truly your garden? Then I want to be the very best garden that I can be.' It was to that end that she asked for both the north and south winds to blow upon her. This seems at first sight to be a puzzling request. Was it not contradictory to invoke winds from opposite directions? Would not the one cancel or negate the other? She is, of course, using the language of poetry, and seen in this way, her request makes perfect sense. Both winds were necessary. The north wind swept away the storm clouds and brought cool, clear weather, while the south wind was warm and laden with moisture. If a garden was to flourish, it needed both of these influences. By calling for both winds, therefore, she was expressing her desire to flourish as a garden.

The wind is used in Scripture as an emblem of the Holy Spirit. In his interview with Nicodemus, the Lord attributed the work of regeneration to the sovereign moving of the Spirit of God and likened this to the wind: 'The wind blows where it wishes, and you hear the sound of it, but cannot tell where it comes from and where it goes. So is everyone who is born of the Spirit' (John 3:8). No one becomes a Christian unless the Spirit of God works in sovereign power in his or her heart. The apostle Paul writes emphatically, 'Those who are in the flesh cannot please God. But you are not in the flesh but in the Spirit, if indeed the Spirit of God dwells in you. Now if anyone does not have the Spirit of Christ, he is not his' (Rom. 8:8-9).

But, thank God, the wind of the Spirit does not cease to blow once we have been regenerated. Taking our cue from the Shulamite, we may speak of the work of the Spirit of God in terms of both a 'north wind' and a 'south wind'. As the former swept away the storms, so the Spirit of God is, upon Christ's people, the wind of conviction and repentance to sweep away the sin in their lives. Equally, as the warm south wind brought comfort and fruitfulness, so the Spirit of God brings comfort, encouragement and spiritual fruit into the life of the church.

It is only as the Spirit ministers to the church in both these ways that the church is truly empowered for the preaching of the gospel. If the north wind of the Spirit is not blowing, the church will compromise her witness to the gospel by a life stained with sin. If the south wind of the Spirit is not blowing, the church will not demonstrate the joy and comfort of knowing Christ, nor will she produce those good works which authenticate the church as God's possession.

What else do the north and south winds accomplish? They spread abroad the fragrance of the garden! The beloved prays, 'Blow upon my garden that its spices may flow out.' Those who are still outside the garden, having no concept of its beauties, need to smell its spices, the rich aroma of its blossom. Here is an unmistakable picture. The fragrance of Christ is spread abroad by the preaching of the gospel in the power of the Spirit. There is no other way for those outside the church to be brought in.

If the fragrance of the gospel is to be wafted to those who do not know the Lord Jesus, both winds must blow. Our sins must be swept away and our comforts and our fruit made evident. The church has much that might make her attractive to unbelievers, but without the preaching of the gospel and the work of the Spirit, they will never know.

The beauty of the church's proclamation of the gospel

The opening words of Solomon's second song of praise, which is found in chapter 7, also compel us to think of the church and the gospel: 'How beautiful are your feet in sandals, O prince's daughter!' (7:1). This compliment may seem strange to us. We do not usually associate feet with beauty, or compliment people on their sandals.

Probably, Solomon's remark should be understood with reference to the 'dance of the double camp', or Mahanaim dance, mentioned in the last verse of chapter 6. Stuart Olyott says this dance was 'presumably a well-known and attractive dance, whose movements required a high degree of concentration from the spectators'.[3] If the Shulamite were performing this dance as Solomon spoke, it makes sense for Solomon to comment on her feet and shoes, and to describe her legs, in Olyott's words, as being 'as graceful in movement as a jewelled pendulum'.[4]

The delight of those who hear the gospel

The spiritual application of Solomon's admiration is, of course, to the feet of the gospel messenger, which in a very real sense 'bring' the gospel! The prophet Isaiah introduces this idea, and Paul takes it up in Romans 10:15. Isaiah was enabled by the Spirit of God to peer into the future of his nation. It was a grim sight. His people were going to be torn violently from their homeland to spend seventy years in captivity in Babylon. But Isaiah's glimpse into the future did not end there. He was able to look beyond that bleak time to a glorious future. He could see his people, there in Babylon, when suddenly a messenger appears on the horizon. This is the messenger the people have been expecting. He carries the good news that they have finally been released from their captivity and can at last return to their homeland. Isaiah describes it in this way:

How beautiful upon the mountains
Are the feet of him who brings good news,
Who proclaims peace,

Who brings glad tidings of good things,
Who proclaims salvation,
Who says to Zion,
'Your God reigns!'

(Isa. 52:7).

It was not, of course, the feet themselves that were beautiful. They would undoubtedly have been covered with dust and would have been most unsightly. But on this grand occasion they were transformed. Their natural ugliness meant nothing. They were now beautiful because they carried the messenger who carried the good news of deliverance. The prophet Nahum refers to the same event in these words:

Behold, on the mountains
The feet of him who brings good tidings,
Who proclaims peace!

(Nahum 1:15).

Deliverance from captivity in Babylon was indeed a thrilling experience for the people of God, but it pales in comparison to another deliverance. Scripture tells us that by nature we are enslaved to Satan (Eph. 2:1-3), but through the gospel we are released from that bondage. With this in mind, the apostle Paul seizes upon Isaiah's words and applies them to the preaching of the gospel. He writes, 'How beautiful are the feet of those who preach the gospel of peace, who bring glad tidings of good things!' (Rom. 10:15).

How true this is! Paul reminds the Galatians that when he brought the gospel to them, they received him 'as an angel of God'. So enthralled were they with the message of salvation through Christ that they were blind to his physical weakness (Gal. 4:13-15). So it should always be. The preacher's shortcomings should be swallowed up in the glory of the message that he brings. Believers, at least, should be so carried away with the beauty of the message that the frailty of the messenger is forgotten. Oh that we had more such preaching today!

In another passage the apostle carried the imagery of the church's feet a step further. The gospel armour in which God's people are to be clad includes shoes which represent 'the preparation of the gospel of peace' (Eph. 6:15). The military sandals worn by Roman soldiers had both an offensive and a defensive purpose. Because their soles were studded with sharp nails, they enabled the soldiers to traverse difficult terrain quickly and take their enemies by surprise. When the soldiers were themselves under attack their sandals kept them from slipping and falling. In like manner, the believer in Christ should be prepared to invade hostile territory with the gospel that brings peace and reconciliation between an offended God and sinful men. It is not so much the gospel that Paul likens to sandals, as our preparedness, or readiness, to *preach* that gospel. Those who know the peace that only the gospel of Christ can give have a readiness to share that peace with others. At the same time, and by that same peace, they are enabled to stand against the onslaughts of Satan.

The delight of the Lord

We shall never truly delight in the gospel ourselves until we understand that Christ himself delights in the church's preaching of the gospel. The beloved in the Song of Solomon is a type of Christ, and it is the beloved who speaks of the beauty of the Shulamite's feet. The Song makes it clear that there were others who observed her dancing and took pleasure in it (6:13), but the emphasis is on the beloved's praise of her. While those who hear the good news of salvation delight in that proclamation, the Lord Jesus Christ delights in it even more.

The gospel is, after all, the work of the triune God. It is the product of God the Father, God the Son and God the Holy Spirit, covenanting together to provide a way for sinners to be redeemed from the ravages of sin. It is, as the apostle Paul termed it on more than one occasion, 'the gospel of God' (1 Thess. 2:2,9; 1 Tim. 1:11). This gospel called for the Second Person of the Trinity to take our humanity and to dwell among us. When the Lord Jesus Christ complied with this plan, and stepped onto the stage of human history, he came preaching the gospel (Matt. 4:23; 9:35; Mark 1:14). He himself said in the synagogue of Nazareth:

> The Spirit of the Lord is upon me,
> Because he has anointed me to preach the gospel to the poor.
> He has sent me to heal the broken-hearted,
> To preach deliverance to the captives
> And recovery of sight to the blind,
> To set at liberty those who are oppressed,
> To preach the acceptable year of the Lord
>
> (Luke 4:18-19).

And when he had finished his redeeming work and was ready to return to the Father, he gave this word of instruction to his disciples: 'Go into all the world and preach the gospel to every creature' (Mark 16:15). It is this same Christ who through his inspired apostle pronounces a fearful curse upon those who dare to pervert his gospel: 'But even if we, or an angel from heaven, preach any other gospel to you than what we have preached to you, let him be accursed' (Gal. 1:8). He jealously guards his gospel against its enemies.

In the light of all these things, there can be no doubt whatever that the Lord Jesus Christ takes immense delight in the feet of his church — that is, in her proclamation of his glorious gospel.

The gospel preached

Christ's delight in the preached gospel is reflected in the sense of privilege displayed by the apostle Paul: 'Therefore we are ambassadors for Christ, as though God were pleading through us: we implore you on Christ's behalf, be reconciled to God' (2 Cor. 5:20). God himself, suggests Paul, is the ultimate preacher, for it is ultimately he who calls men to repentance, faith and reconciliation. The church and its servants are merely ambassadors, carrying the message of the King into all the world.

We have, then, brought together three images used by the beloved in the Song of Solomon, and related them to the church's work of preaching the gospel. The fountains of living water, the wind-borne spices of the garden and the feet of the beloved — all these testify to the church's privilege and responsibility to take the gospel to every creature. If we need further justification for using this imagery in this way, we have only to look at the closing verses of Psalm 147. There we find running feet, wind and water used as emblems of God's Word going forth. Let the psalmist, therefore, have the last word on this important subject:

> He sends out his command to the earth;
> His word runs very swiftly...
> He sends out his word...
> He causes his wind to blow, and the waters flow
> > (Ps. 147:15,18).

15.
The church triumphant

'O my love, you are as beautiful as Tirzah, lovely as Jerusa-
lem, awesome as an army with banners!'
(S. of S. 6:4; cf. 6:10).

In his second song in praise of his bride, Solomon twice draws
a remarkable analogy. She is, he declares, 'awesome as an
army with banners'. A bride today would hardly consider this
a compliment! It might, indeed, be a way to describe a par-
ticularly contentious and belligerent spouse. Yet we may be
sure that the Shulamite took it as a tribute and had no doubts
about what her beloved was saying.

In those days an army assembled under its various banners
would have been a stately and majestic sight. By using this
figure Solomon was paying the Shulamite a very high compliment indeed. Hers was such a dignified and awesome beauty
that those around her were compelled to take notice of it and
be impressed by it. Solomon's comparison of his bride to an
army quite naturally leads the Christian to think of the church
in the same terms.

The church militant

Until recent times, Christians have for centuries delighted to
think of the church in military terms. Older hymnals were well
stocked with hymns calling attention to this aspect of the Christian life. Perhaps the best known of such hymns is 'Onward
Christian Soldiers':

Onward Christian soldiers,
Marching as to war,
With the cross of Jesus
Going on before!
Christ, the royal Master,
Leads against the foe;
Forward into battle,
See his banner go!

(Sabine Baring-Gould)

Such hymns have now fallen into disfavour. Some insist that Christians should oppose anything that seems to smack of violence. Others see the Christian life as the way to secure health and wealth and, because the military motif suggests hardship and sacrifice, have no place for it in their thinking.

No matter how distasteful and disconcerting we may find this military language, the fact is that it features quite prominently in the Scriptures. We may summarize the biblical teaching on this matter under the following heads.

The church's spiritual warfare

The apostle Paul was keenly conscious of being engaged in spiritual warfare, and he knew that what was true of him as an individual was also true of the whole church. He sets out the reality of spiritual warfare in several places. In his letter to the Ephesians, he exhorts: 'Put on the whole armour of God, that you may be able to stand against the wiles of the devil. For we do not wrestle against flesh and blood, but against principalities, against powers, against the rulers of the darkness of this age, against spiritual hosts of wickedness in the heavenly places' (Eph. 6:11-12).

The warfare of the church stems from the fact that she has a great adversary, Satan. Originally known as Lucifer, he was filled with pride and rebelled against God (Isa. 14:12-15). That rebellion led to his being cast out of heaven, along with all those angels who supported him. Since then he has busied himself ceaselessly in opposing God at every turn. Because he is opposed to God he is also opposed to the people of God.

Paul's words to the Ephesians indicate something of the nature of the warfare Satan conducts against God's people. First, the devil often resorts to 'wiles' in this warfare. He can prowl and roar like the lion (1 Peter 5:8), but he generally prefers to rely on deception. So effective is he at this that the apostles repeatedly found it necessary to remind the churches, 'Be not deceived,' or 'Let no one deceive you' (1 Cor. 15:33; Gal. 6:7; Eph 5:6; 2 Thess. 2:3; 1 John 3:7; cf. 1 Cor. 3:18; James 1:22; 1 John 1:8).

When Paul writes of 'principalities' and 'powers', he seems to refer to the power and authority attained by those angels who joined Satan in his rebellion. His reference to the 'rulers of the darkness of this age' indicates that the spiritual and moral darkness of this world must be explained in terms of the control exerted by these satanic forces. It is Satan, he says, who has blinded the minds of those who do not believe and from whom the gospel is hidden (2 Cor. 4:3-4).

The phrase 'spiritual hosts of wickedness' emphasizes both the number and the nature of the satanic forces. A single 'host' is a significant number, but these armies consist of many 'hosts', and they are totally devoted to evil. John Eadie says their 'appetite for evil only exceeds their capability for producing it'.[1] In addition to these details, Paul tells us that Satan's hosts occupy 'the heavenly places', which is his way of stressing the supernatural and superhuman nature of these evil spirits.

Later in his description of the Christian's spiritual armour, Paul refers to the 'fiery darts of the wicked one' (Eph. 6:16). These may very well refer to sudden, fierce attacks of Satan. They may come in the form of blasphemous thoughts, doubts, evil imaginations that crop up suddenly in the mind and seem to stick there, and many other similar things.

Many people scoff at such details because they cannot see the hand of Satan in these things. In doing so, they succumb to the wiles of the devil. He is never happier than when he is thought not to exist. But exist he does, and because he does the church is engaged in fierce warfare every day of her life in this world.

One of the primary weapons Satan wields in his warfare against the church is false teaching. The apostle Paul was finely tuned to this stratagem and incessantly warned the churches regarding it. He told the Corinthians that 'Satan transforms himself into an angel of light' and that his followers were similarly able to 'transform themselves into ministers of righteousness' (2 Cor. 11:14-15). As he was taking his leave of the Ephesian elders, he warned them that 'savage wolves' would come among them who would not spare the flock, but would instead speak 'perverse things' (Acts 20:29-30).

He also cautioned the Christians in Philippi against those who were 'enemies of the cross of Christ' (Phil. 3:18). Again and again the apostle sounded the alarm. He called young ministers, like Timothy and Titus, to be ever watchful against false teachers (1 Tim. 1:3-7,18-20; 4:1-5; 6:3-11; 2 Tim. 1:15; 2:17-18; 3:6-9,13; Titus 1:10-16). He urged them above all things to teach and cultivate 'sound doctrine' (1 Tim. 1:10; 2 Tim. 4:3; Titus 1:9; 2:1). It is important for us to realize that Paul was not alone in this concern. Peter, John, Jude and the author of Hebrews all sounded the same alarm (Heb. 13:9; 2 Peter 2:1-3,14-19; 1 John 4:1-3; 2 John 7-11; Jude 4,8-11).

We cannot leave the warfare that Satan wages against the church without calling attention to its focal point. There is nothing Satan hates more than the cross of Christ. That cross declares and represents truths he simply cannot tolerate. It proclaims that man is a sinner, that his sin is a very serious matter, that it deserves the condemnation of hell and that man can do nothing about it for himself. But, thank God, the cross of Christ also triumphantly announces that God has judged both sin and Satan through the shed blood of his Son and that there is, therefore, no condemnation to those who are in Christ Jesus.

The cross trumpets the truths of God's holiness, man's sin and atonement through the blood of Christ — together, of course, with that of Christ's victory over sin and death and the powers of darkness. Satan fiercely hates each one of these truths, let alone their cumulative effect and message. He works ceaselessly, therefore, to send into this world false teachers who are 'enemies of the cross of Christ' (Phil. 3:19), who corrupt men's minds from 'the simplicity that is in Christ' (2 Cor. 11:3) and who declare 'another Jesus' and 'a different gospel' (2 Cor. 11:4; Gal. 1:6-7).

What are we to do? It is an intimidating thing to read about the malevolent designs of Satan and the subtlety, power and ferocity with which he attacks the church. We find ourselves wondering how the church can ever hope to survive in such a war, let alone win it. But Scripture holds before us great truths to encourage and comfort us, and this is certainly true of our passage in the Song of Solomon.

The church has a captain

As every army has a general, so the church also has a leader. In Scripture this leader is sometimes called her 'captain', and this captain is Christ himself. In Hebrews he is described as 'the captain of their salvation' through whom God is 'bringing many sons unto glory' (Heb. 2:10, AV). The word can also be translated 'chief captain' or 'author'. A leader's fame is in proportion to his victories. How great will be his fame, then, and how great a victory it will be, when Christ leads his ransomed hosts into the city of heaven, the glorious kingdom prepared for them from the foundation of the world! (Matt. 25:34). This captain cannot fail, for his final triumph was assured in the eternal counsels of Almighty God.

In Old Testament times, Joshua also learned that he had a captain. He thought he was the leader of the armies of Israel, and so he was in a purely human sense. But as he surveyed the fortress of Jericho, which stood as a barrier to the land of promise, he suddenly saw a man 'with his sword drawn in his hand' (Josh. 5:13). 'Are you for us or for our adversaries?', challenged Joshua sternly, ready to do battle. How unprepared he was for the reply! 'As Commander [AV, captain] of the army of the LORD I have now come', said the stranger, who went on to say, 'Take your sandal off your foot, for the place where you stand is holy.' Joshua did as he was told and, falling on his face, worshipped him (Josh. 5:14-15).

There can be little doubt that what Joshua experienced was a 'theophany' — that is, an Old Testament appearance of God in human form — or that the one who appeared to him was Christ, the Son of God. Why did he appear? Read on into chapter 6 of Joshua and all becomes clear. The Lord went on to give Joshua full instructions for the siege and destruction of Jericho. Who, then, was leading the armies of the Lord? It was not Joshua, but Christ.

What was true then is doubly true today. We may feel we battle against unequal odds, but the one who leads the church in its warfare is Christ, the Son of God, to whom all power has been given in heaven and on earth.

The church has been given a banner

The church of Jesus Christ is like an army with banners. The army of the nation of Israel marched under several banners

(Num. 2:1-31;10:14-28), which were a means of rallying them to the cause and organizing them for battle. The church's 'banners' are in fact but one, the plural implying the excellence of that single ensign. The following words from a psalm of David suggest the nature of that banner: 'You have given a banner to those who fear you, that it may be displayed because of the truth' (Ps. 60:4).

David may have been referring to his own leadership of Israel. His reign was indeed a rallying point, a unifying and energizing force for the nation. Furthermore, as David grew in strength and influence he became a source of terror to all the enemies of Israel. However, the psalm expressly tells us that the banner is one of truth. In other words, in the gospel of Jesus Christ, the church has a far greater banner than David was to Israel, and it is of the gospel that the psalm speaks prophetically. That gospel is the truth of God and it displays God's faithfulness to his truth. It unifies and energizes the church and, yes, it disconcerts and dismays those who are opposed to Christ. The church marches under that banner as she proclaims the good news of salvation through her crucified Redeemer.

The church has been given armour

In addition to having a captain and a banner, the church has been given armour that protects her from Satan and the forces of wickedness. The apostle Paul details this armour in Ephesians 6:10-17. He calls it the armour of God (Eph. 6:11). It is God who provides it. If the church were to fight in her own strength, she would most certainly be mortally wounded, but in God's armour she succeeds in her battle and is safe. Some of the armour is defensive in nature.

The girdle of truth

Before she can ever hope to resist Satan, the church must be settled in her convictions. She must rest in confidence that she has the truth that was 'once for all delivered to the saints' (Jude 3). There is no hope for success in spiritual warfare if the church thinks that truth is never certain but ever changing.

The breastplate of righteousness

The central tenet of the gospel is this: guilty sinners can stand in the presence of the holy God by being clothed in the perfect righteousness of the Lord Jesus Christ. The imputed righteousness of Christ gives rise to an imparted righteousness, by which I mean that God's people, as they are sanctified by the Spirit of God, practise righteousness. One of the ways Satan attacks the church is by sowing seeds of doubt. Those who make up the church can withstand the onslaught of doubt by pointing to the perfect righteousness of the Lord Jesus Christ.

The feet shod with the preparation of the gospel of peace

The shoes, as we noted in the previous chapter, call attention to firmness of footing and readiness to move forward. The peace created by the gospel — peace with God, peace with others and peace within — enables the people of God to stand against the anxieties Satan hurls in their path. That same peace gives the children of God an eagerness to share the gospel with others.

The shield of faith

This shield is given by God to enable his people to quench Satan's 'fiery darts'. Those darts, as we have already seen, refer to any sudden attack from Satan that causes wicked, ungodly thoughts or fears to crop up in the mind and stick there. The Christian wields the shield of faith when he counters such attacks, pointing Satan to the complete adequacy of the Lord Jesus Christ and relying on the revealed character of God and the promises of God.

The helmet of salvation

In his first letter to the Thessalonians, the apostle Paul designates this helmet as 'the hope of salvation' (1 Thess. 5:8). Satan loves to discourage the church by suggesting that she is engaged in a futile enterprise. Believers take up the helmet of salvation when they fortify their minds with the promises of God regarding the future. Those promises assure us that the Lord Jesus Christ will gather every last one of his elect, that he will return to take his people home and that they will then be finally and completely vindicated.

The church has been given a weapon

After listing the defensive parts of the armour, Paul proceeds to call attention to the weapon the church is given — namely, 'the sword of the Spirit, which is the word of God' (Eph. 6:17). The Word of God is, for the church, a weapon both of defence and offence. By relying on its teachings, she can fend off Satan's attacks. By wielding it in proclamation, she can put him and his forces to flight.

The classic example of this is, of course, Satan's temptation of the Lord Jesus Christ in the wilderness. Three times Satan tempted Jesus, and each time our Lord responded by saying, 'It is written...' (Matt. 4:4,7,10). The writings to which he was referring were, of course, the Scriptures, which he proceeded to quote on each occasion. The account closes by saying, 'Then the devil left him... ' (Matt. 4:11). If we will follow the Lord's example we may expect the same result.

The Word of God is a very powerful and potent weapon. The author of Hebrews describes it in these terms: 'For the word of God is living and powerful, and sharper than any two-edged sword, piercing even to the division of soul and spirit, and of joints and marrow, and is a discerner of the thoughts and intents of the heart' (Heb. 4:12). As the church employs this powerful weapon, she will see Satan's 'strongholds', his fortifications, pulled down. All the arguments Satan sows in the minds of sinners, arguments they use to exalt themselves against the knowledge of God, will be cast down. Through the power of the Word of God, the church can expect to see such sinners captured and brought into obedience of Christ (2 Cor. 10:4-5).

The church has been given the privilege of prayer

It is interesting that Paul concludes his description of the Christian's armour by urging his readers to pray 'always with all prayer and supplication in the Spirit' (Eph. 6:18). Some have wondered why Paul did not include prayer as one of the items in the Christian's armoury. Is this not a serious oversight? There is a perfectly good reason why he did not do so. He wanted to emphasize that the whole armour is to be taken up and employed in a prayerful manner. Every single piece of armour and every weapon is to be polished or honed with prayer.

When Paul speaks of prayer, he is not talking about the casual, nonchalant muttering of words. He is calling for prayer that is sincere and fervent. One cannot be casual about warfare! Warfare-praying has certain dimensions to it. It first requires us to use 'all prayer' — that is, every form of prayer.

Prayers of thanksgiving, supplication, petition and intercession all play a vital role in our combat against Satan, as do public and private prayer. The apostle especially calls for 'supplication' as the key form of praying. We cannot succeed in our warfare unless we beseech God to supply the strength and resolve that we so greatly need.

Secondly, this praying is to be 'always'. We are to 'pray without ceasing' (1 Thess. 5:17). This cannot mean that Christians are to do nothing else but pray. That is impossible, for Scripture clearly assigns other responsibilities to us as well. But whatever we do is to be done in an attitude of prayer and with a readiness to resort to prayer.

All of this, moreover, is to be 'in the Spirit'. We are to recognize our helplessness and weakness apart from God, and depend on the Spirit to give us the spirit of prayer — that is, to help us to formulate our petitions and to offer them in faith, and to give us the warmth and fervency that effective prayer requires.

How the teaching of the apostle challenges and rebukes us! Most Christians have much to lament here, and much to learn. We are engaged in a most fearful warfare against a dreadful adversary, but our praying is often spasmodic, half-hearted and haphazard. Fortunately, we are also assured that our God occupies a throne of grace and that through prayer we can freely approach that throne to 'obtain mercy and find grace to help in time of need' (Heb. 4:16).

From time to time we hear accounts of individuals living as paupers while they have a fortune laid aside. We shake our heads in wonderment at such accounts. But many Christians are doing something very similar in the spiritual realm when they fail to draw upon Christ's riches at the throne of grace, through the privilege of prayer. The church has always made her greatest advances when she most vigorously gave herself to prayer. Satan is not impressed with our personalities and our attempts to attract people by offering them a range of church activities. But when the army of Christ's church prays, the earth trembles beneath its tread and Satan flees.

The church has been given a promise

As we looked at the shield of faith and the helmet of salvation, we noticed how important it is for the church to rely on the promises of God. There are indeed many precious and wonderful promises upon which she may draw in her combat with satanic forces, but perhaps none is more needed than the promise which the Lord Jesus gave to his disciples at Caesarea Philippi. After Simon Peter affirmed that he, Jesus, was indeed the Son of the living God, the Lord said, 'On this rock I will build my church, and the gates of Hades shall not prevail against it' (Matt. 16:18).

Satan sends out all kinds of schemes and designs, and they stream outwards, as it were, through the gates of hell. These schemes are so diabolically deceitful and evil that it often seems that they will succeed, and the church will fail. But the Lord Jesus Christ, who is the foundation of the church, has guaranteed that they will not succeed. No matter what plans the devil hatches and sends out through the gates of hell, the church will prevail. Secure in that promise, the church can continue to march under the banner of her Lord and fight Satan effectively. As she does so, she is lovely to her Lord, an army with banners; and she is terrifying to Satan.

16.
Christ's love fulfilled

> ' *Set me as a seal upon your heart, as a seal upon your*
> *arm; for love is as strong as death...* ' (S. of S. 8:6).

It is difficult to determine at what point in the Song the wedding of Solomon and the Shulamite takes place. Some put it as early as the third chapter (3:6-11). Others contend that this is only the Shulamite dreaming of their forthcoming wedding, and that the happy couple are finally joined together in the passage which runs from chapter 7:1 - 8:7, and to which we now turn. Whatever view one takes on this matter, it is evident that the emphasis in these verses is on the fulfilment, or consummation, of the love of the beloved and his bride.

Expressions of fulfilment

This section of the Song overflows with pictures and expressions of fulfilment, provided both by Solomon and by his bride.

Solomon

One expression of fulfilment is found in the following words from the lips of Solomon: 'I will go up to the palm tree, I will take hold of its branches' (7:8). Solomon has just described the beauty of his bride. He has likened her stature to a palm tree and her breasts to clusters of the vine (7:7). In announcing his intention to 'go up to the palm tree' and 'take hold of its branches', Solomon is proclaiming his desire to engage in love-making with his wife. This is the language of physical intimacy.

The Shulamite

The emphasis on consummation continues when the Shulamite refers to the mandrakes emitting their fragrance (7:13). The mandrake was a plant with purple flowers and a tomato-like fruit that was orange in colour. The ancients considered it to be an aphrodisiac (Gen. 30:14-16). The Shulamite also makes mention of the 'pleasant fruits' that were at their gates, fruits that she had 'laid up' for her beloved (7:13). She has reserved sexual intimacy for her husband, and the time has now come for her to share herself with him.

The Shulamite continues to use the language of intimacy saying, 'His left hand is under my head, and his right hand embraces me' (8:3). She charges the daughters of Jerusalem not to disturb them until their lovemaking is over (8:4). The emphasis on the consummation of their love comes to an end with the bride speaking to her beloved about the strength of love: 'Love is as strong as death... Many waters cannot quench love, nor can the floods drown it' (8:6-7).

A future consummation

What possible relevance could this emphasis on physical intimacy and fulfilment have to the Lord Jesus Christ and his church? The answer is that the Bible speaks of a day of spiritual consummation and heavenly fulfilment in Christ's relationship with his church. This is the day to which all things have been pointing and tending from eternity past.

Just as both Solomon and the Shulamite eagerly anticipated the consummation of their relationship, so Christ and his church look forward to the consummation of theirs. That will be the day when the church will finally enter his presence to receive the end of her salvation, and he will receive her as his bride.

In his letter to the Ephesians, the apostle Paul refers to this consummation as an inheritance. His words reveal, in fact, a twofold inheritance. First, there is the inheritance of the saints, and second, the inheritance of Christ. The word 'inheritance' appears three times in Ephesians 1:1-18. In verse 11 the apostle says, 'We have obtained an inheritance.' In verse 14 he refers to the Holy Spirit as 'the guarantee of our inheritance'. In verse 18 the phrase 'his inheritance in the saints' appears.

Scholars are divided on the first and last of these phrases. Some think they refer to the inheritance the church will receive, while others understand them to refer to the church as the inheritance Christ receives. No matter how we interpret these two expressions, it is quite evident that Paul had both the church's inheritance and Christ's inheritance in mind. Both aspects are indicated by the apostle in verse 14, the former by the words 'our inheritance', and the latter by the phrase 'the redemption of the purchased possession'.

The word 'possession' takes us back to those Old Testament passages that teach that Israel was God's possession, or heritage (Exod. 19:5; Deut. 7:6; 14:2; 26:18; Isa. 43:20-21; Ezek. 37:23; Mal. 3:17). These scriptures undergird Paul's claim that the church, with both her Jewish and Gentile members, is the true possession, or heritage, of God. Other New Testament writers affirm the same truth by calling those who make up the church God's 'own special people' (Titus 2:14; 1 Peter 2:9). We can legitimately speak, then, of both the church and Christ as receiving an inheritance.

The inheritance of the church

In this world the church receives, in all their fulness, the spiritual blessings that God has bestowed upon her (Eph. 1:3). Yet a greater fulness is in store. In the life to come, she will receive the ultimate fruition of her faith, and will do so amidst the glories of heaven.

The apostle Peter offers praise to God for this inheritance in these words: 'Blessed be the God and Father of our Lord Jesus Christ, who according to his abundant mercy has begotten us again to a living hope through the resurrection of Jesus Christ from the dead, to an inheritance incorruptible and undefiled and that does not fade away, reserved in heaven for you, who are kept by the power of God through faith for salvation ready to be revealed in the last time' (1 Peter 1:3-5).

These verses brim with truths that clamour for attention. First, they contain a description of the inheritance that awaits the church. It is incorruptible, undefiled and unfading.

The word 'incorruptible' means it is incapable of perishing. It is indestructible. This world is passing away (1 John 2:17), but the church's inheritance will endure for ever.

The inheritance is also 'undefiled'. Inheritances in this world are often defiled. The nation of Israel received the land of Canaan, but it was a defiled inheritance. The Canaanites had defiled it with their iniquity, and Israel herself defiled it with idolatry. This whole world bears the taint of sin, and the stench of sin is everywhere apparent. But the inheritance of the church will never be spoiled or polluted. It will be for ever free from the blemish of sin.

It is, finally, an 'unfading' inheritance. We know what it is for something to grow old even though it endures. Our bodies grow old and weaken even though they are still alive. Buildings deteriorate while they are still standing. But the inheritance awaiting the church will never fade or tarnish. It will not only endure for ever, but will do so without diminishing or deteriorating. Ten million years in glory will not lessen the glory.

Another element of Peter's statement that cries out for attention is the dual 'keeping' to which he refers. He tells us that the inheritance is 'reserved in heaven' for those who 'are kept by the power of God through faith' (1 Peter 1:4-5). In other words, he says that the inheritance is kept *for believers,* and that they are kept *for it.*

This removes all uncertainty about the fact that the church will receive her inheritance. The inheritance itself cannot be destroyed, nor can those for whom it is prepared. It should not escape our notice that God's keeping of his people is 'through faith'. The way God keeps his people is by continuing to kindle faith within, so that they continue to believe in him, love him and serve him.

And, of course, all of this flows from the grace of God. The church does not receive this inheritance because of any merit or work of her own. God begets us to this inheritance. He quickens us while we are in our sins and plants 'a living hope' in us, and he does so through the redeeming work of his Son, Jesus Christ (1 Peter 1:3). Peter's brief review of this inheritance is only a sample of what Scripture has to say about it. There is much more.

The apostle Paul offers insight into the day on which the church will receive this inheritance. On that day the Lord Jesus Christ will return from heaven to raise the bodies of all his people who have died and to translate instantaneously those of his people who are still alive (1 Thess. 4:13-18). The coming of Christ for his bride is also anticipated prophetically in Psalm 45. There we find the bridegroom has gone away to his palace to prepare for his wedding day. The bride is at home doing the same and also awaiting her beloved's return. As she waits she passes the time by rehearsing his many delightful qualities (Ps. 45:2-9). At long last the wait is over. The king leaves his ivory palaces (Ps. 45:8) and makes his way to where his bride is waiting. Her attendants rush out to meet him and excitedly announce that she is ready. The New King James Version has them saying, 'The royal daughter is all glorious within *the palace*' (Ps. 45:13). The words in italics were not in the original, but have been supplied by the translators. In most cases, such added words help the sense of a passage, but in this case they give a mistaken impression. The bride was not in the palace, but at her own home, and the king came to her from his palace. The church, which is pictured here, does not wait for her Lord in a palace, but rather in this dark world.

The attendants proceed to assure the king that his bride is fully prepared for his arrival, that she has attired herself in clothing 'woven with gold' and that she will soon be presented to him in 'robes of many colours' (Ps. 45:13-14).

When the Lord comes to claim his bride he will find her arrayed in the clothing that he himself provided for her, the garment of his perfect righteousness. And he will also find that she has been prepared by the sanctifying work of the Holy Spirit so that she has, in addition to the garment of perfect righteousness, an inner beauty about her. That moment of meeting will be followed by the procession back to the king's palace and to the marriage feast. It will indeed be a time of 'gladness and rejoicing'.

In the book of Revelation the apostle John relates what he had heard spoken by 'a loud voice of a great multitude in heaven'. The words are amazingly similar to those we have just noted in Psalm 45. That voice said, ' "Let us be glad and rejoice and give him glory, for the marriage of the Lamb has come, and his wife has made herself ready." And to her it was granted to be arrayed in fine linen, clean and bright, for the fine linen is the righteous acts of the saints' (Rev. 19:7-8). Then John heard a voice from the throne of heaven say, 'Blessed are those who are called to the marriage supper of the Lamb!' (Rev. 19:9).

This, then, is something of what comes to mind when we read of the church's 'inheritance'. But as we return to the words of the apostle Paul in the first chapter of Ephesians, we find that there is another aspect to this word. In addition to the saints' inheritance, there is also Christ's inheritance.

The fulfilment of Christ's love for the church

The terms in which Paul refers to the future inheritance have been the subject of a significant debate. Some think the apostle's phrase, 'We have obtained an inheritance' (Eph. 1:11) should be translated, 'We were made a heritage.' If this were the case, the apostle would not be calling attention to what the church will inherit, but rather to what Christ himself will inherit.

The phrase can be translated either way, and we cannot determine which emphasis Paul had in mind with that particular phrase. The same is true of the expression Paul uses in verse 18: 'his inheritance in the saints'. John Stott explains: 'The Greek expression, like the English, could mean either God's inheritance or ours, that is, either the inheritance he receives or the inheritance he bestows.'[1]

Having said that, Stott proceeds to choose the latter. He writes, 'But the parallel passage in Colossians 1:12 strongly suggests the other interpretation here, namely that "God's inheritance" refers to what he will give us.'[2] But even if we take each usage of the word 'inheritance' in Ephesians 1 to refer to the inheritance the church will eventually receive, there is in that same passage one phrase that clearly indicates that Christ also receives an inheritance — that is, the church herself. In Ephesians 1:14 the apostle speaks of 'the redemption of the purchased possession'.

Several scriptures affirm that the church is already Christ's inheritance. The people of God in the Old Testament are considered to be his special possession (Exod. 19:5; 23:22; Deut. 7:6; 14:2; 26:18; Isa. 43:20-21; Ezek. 37:23; Mal. 3:17). The New Testament writers affirm the same by calling those who make up the church God's own special people (Titus 2:14; 1 Peter 2:9). But while the church is already Christ's prized possession, she will be even more so when he receives her unto himself. To understand and appreciate what it means for Christ to receive the church as his inheritance we have to follow Paul as he looks at the glorious panorama of the plan of redemption

It began in eternity past. That is where the church was born. There, before ever the world was created, God the Father gave to God the Son the church to be his bride. The apostle Paul says, 'Blessed be the God and Father of our Lord Jesus Christ, who has blessed us with every spiritual blessing in the heavenly places in Christ, just as he chose us in him before the foundation of the world, that we should be holy and without blame before him in love, having predestined us to adoption as sons by Jesus Christ to himself, according to the good pleasure of his will' (Eph. 1:3-5).

In receiving this gift from his Father, the Son agreed to do something — namely, to redeem her. The church he was to receive from the Father would consist of individuals who were sinners by nature, and the Lord Jesus Christ, who is holy and perfect, could not take a bride besmirched and stained by sin. What was necessary for Christ to redeem his church, so that he could take her as his bride? The apostle gives us the answer. He tells us that in Christ, 'We have redemption through his blood, the forgiveness of sins, according to the riches of his grace' (Eph. 1:7).

It was by shedding his blood on the cross that the Lord Jesus redeemed his church from her sin. He took her place and received the penalty for her sin that God's justice demanded. In taking that penalty, he exhausted the wrath of God against her, so that there is now no penalty left for her to pay. Paul celebrates this glorious deed by saying, 'Christ also loved the church and gave himself for it' (Eph. 5:25).

All of this was to be undertaken with one grand moment in mind — that moment in which Christ will present the church to himself as 'a glorious church, not having spot or wrinkle or any such thing' (Eph. 5:27). At that moment, the plan of redemption will reach its fulfilment. That plan, contrived so long ago, and executed over such a long period of time, will at last be consummated.

This glorious consummation inevitably raises the question: what will it mean for us? Scripture would have us also think of what it will mean for Christ! F. F. Bruce writes, 'We can scarcely realize what it must mean to God to see his purpose complete, to see creatures of his hand, sinners redeemed by his grace, reflecting his own glory.'[3]

The satisfaction we experience in our daily lives over achieving a planned goal can only be the very faintest indication of the satisfaction the triune God will know in seeing the fulfilment of the greatest of all plans. Christ will receive the bride that he loved from eternity and purchased in history. The bride given to him by the Father, and called to him by the Holy Spirit, will then be his, and his for ever. And he will be absolutely delighted with her.

As we look at this world, and at the church limping along in this world, we might fear that God's plan to give his Son a people is dangling precariously by a tattered thread. That is what Satan would have us to believe, but it is not so. God's plan will not fail. When the Lord Jesus finally takes to himself the people the Father gave him, not one will be missing. The bride will be complete. And she will not disappoint Christ. The Lord will not receive a bride spattered with the mud of iniquity and dressed in the tattered rags of sin. The plan of redemption will not produce a deficient church and a dejected Christ. It will rather yield to our Lord a complete bride who is perfectly fair. And the one who loved her, with a love surpassing comprehension, will be ecstatic over her.

17.
Longing for daybreak

'Until the day breaks and the shadows flee away...'
(S. of S. 2:17; 4:6).

My heart would not let me leave this wonderful Song of Solomon without calling attention to the sublime words that head this chapter. The Shulamite first uses these words after she and her beloved had been separated (2:17). That agonizing separation finally came to an end when he suddenly came to her again. As she mused on that visit, the bride realized how much like a gazelle her beloved had been in bringing that separation to an end. The gazelle is a very speedy animal with great leaping ability, and her beloved, in gazelle-like fashion, had come to her as quickly as possible and had leaped over difficult circumstances and formidable obstacles to do so.

As she reflected on this experience she realized there would be other periods of separation, periods in which she would again feel the shadows of sadness steal over her. So she pleads with her beloved to visit her as frequently as possible until that day came when they would never have to be separated again.

Look at the words of her petition in verse 17, where she makes reference to the mountains of Bether. The word 'Bether' signifies division or separation. In the words of James Durham, the bride was saying, 'So long ... as these mountains divide [between] me and thee ... be not a stranger, but swiftly, easily, and kindly ... come thou to me, and comfort me with frequent love-visits, until that time come, that thou take me to thee, to enjoy thee fully and immediately.'[1]

The beloved himself also uses this statement in his song of praise to the Shulamite. He pledges to busy himself gathering spices to heap upon his bride 'until the day breaks and the shadows flee' (4:6). Christians surely cannot read these words without thinking of three glorious daybreaks.

The day of Christ's first coming

Scripture often speaks of Christ's first coming to this earth as the breaking of day. The prophets spoke of it in this way. Isaiah pictured his people as being in a state of 'trouble and darkness, gloom of anguish' (Isa. 8:22). But that was not the end of the story. Gloom would give way to glorious light:

> The people who walked in darkness
> Have seen a great light;
> Those who dwelt in the land of the shadow of death,
> Upon them a light has shined
>
> > (Isa. 9:2).

Through the prophet Malachi, God delivered this glowing message to the believers of that day:

> But to you who fear my name
> The Sun of Righteousness shall arise
> With healing in his wings;
> And you shall go out
> And grow fat like stall-fed calves
>
> > (Mal. 4:2).

Those prophecies were fulfilled when Jesus came. A short time before he was born Zacharias, the father of John the Baptist, was shown by the Spirit of God that his son would be the forerunner of the Messiah (Luke 1:76). This caused Zacharias to glorify the mercy of God in the following terms.

> ... the Dayspring from on high has visited us;
> To give light to those who sit in darkness and the shadow
> of death,
> To guide our feet into the way of peace
>
> (Luke 1:78-79).

The word 'dayspring' means 'sunrise' or 'dawn', and Zacharias was, therefore, asserting that the coming of the Messiah would dispel darkness and inaugurate a new day.

The day of salvation

Scripture also speaks of the salvation of sinners as the dawning of a new day. We have previously seen the Bible equating sin with darkness. When the sinner is converted, that darkness is dispelled.

When Paul stood before Agrippa, he related how the risen Lord had commanded him to take the gospel to the Gentiles. In those words, the Lord equated salvation with the dissipation of darkness. He was calling Paul to a ministry that was 'to open their eyes and to turn them from darkness to light, and from the power of Satan to God, that they may receive forgiveness of sins' (Acts 26:18).

Writing to the Colossians, Paul thanked God for salvation and described it as deliverance from 'the power of darkness' (Col. 1:13). How does this deliverance come about? Paul puts it like this: 'For it is the God who commanded light to shine out of darkness who has shone in our hearts to give the light of the knowledge of the glory of God in the face of Jesus Christ' (2 Cor. 4:6).

We are delivered from darkness when God causes the light of knowledge to shine in our hearts. We are saved as a result of our minds being enlightened. This is the gift of faith. We are first made aware of God and what he is like. We see that he is the Creator of all things and that he is also the Judge before whom we must stand. We are made to see that he is a holy God who has declared that nothing sinful will ever enter heaven. We further see that we cannot stand before such a holy God, that we have broken his commands, and justly stand under his condemnation, that we have absolutely nothing to offer God and that we can do nothing to commend ourselves to him. All of this delivers a devastating and shattering blow. It drives us to deep, dark despair and, in so doing, makes us ready to receive the glorious news of the gospel.

Our minds are further enlightened to understand the truth about Jesus Christ. We go beyond the mere facts about Jesus to understand that he is the Second Person of the Trinity, who took our humanity that he might render to God the righteous obedience that God demands. He took our humanity also that, in our place, he might suffer God's judgement on our sin. We are enabled to see that because Christ took the penalty for our sin we can receive the imputed righteousness of the Lord Jesus. Our understanding of the grace of God in Christ leads us to renounce our sin and cast ourselves in faith upon the Saviour and his atoning work.

In addition to having our minds enlightened about these matters, we find our hearts are moved. We find ourselves agreeing with, and approving of, God's plan of salvation. We begin to take God's side in the matter of sin. We begin to justify God instead of ourselves. We count ourselves dead to sin and alive to Christ (Rom. 6:11). The darkness of sin, the darkness of guilt and the darkness of fear of judgement relinquish their grip and the sun of salvation rises in our hearts. The day breaks and the shadows flee away.

The eternal day

While the imagery of the shadows fleeing and the day breaking may rightly cause us to think about the coming of the
Lord to this earth, and the coming of salvation to the individual, the primary reference is to the dawning of the eternal day. Then all shadows will completely and permanently
flee away. The prophet Zechariah looks forward to that day
with these words:

> It shall be one day
> Which is known to the LORD —
> Neither day nor night.
> But at evening time it shall happen
> That it will be light
>
> (Zech. 14:7).

This verse looks forward to this whole age in which we are
now living, the age which we might refer to as the gospel age.
It tells us that this age is one in which it will be 'neither day
nor night'. Do we not find ourselves nodding in agreement
with this statement? We know Matthew Henry is right to say,
'We are between hope and fear, not knowing what to make of
things.'[2]

This is not entirely an age of light. There is so much darkness in this world of ours, darkness that makes our hearts ache
and causes us to groan and sigh. Homes fall apart, and we
mourn the darkness of life. Churches grope and stumble along,
and we groan over the darkness of life. Wars break out, and
we sigh over the darkness of life. Millions of babies in the
womb are casually discarded every year, and we despair
over the darkness of life. Drugs, AIDS, pornography, crime
and political corruption scourge mankind, and we sigh over
the darkness.

Yet it is not entirely an age of darkness, because in the midst of darkness we have bright gleams of marvellous light to delight and warm us. We marry the person we love, and we laugh together enjoying the light of life. Children come into our lives, and we rejoice over the light of life. True friends come across our path, and we realize the light of life is shining upon us. Most of us enjoy good health for many years, and that is all part of the light of life.

But we have even greater light than these things. Jesus said, 'I am the light of the world. He who follows me shall not walk in darkness, but have the light of life' (John 8:12). We have the light of God's presence and the light of his promises. It is, therefore, neither an age of complete light nor one of complete darkness. It is an age of twilight.

Thank God, this mixed age will some day come to an end. Zechariah refers to this as 'evening time'. It will be evening time as far as this twilight age is concerned. But it will be dawn as far as the eternal day is concerned. And when the evening of this age comes and the new age dawns, 'It will be light.'

This takes us to the very end of the Bible — and I am happy to be able to say I have read its last chapter. There we find these blessed words: 'There shall be no night there: they need no lamp nor light of the sun, for the Lord God gives them light. And they shall reign for ever and ever' (Rev. 22:5). What is this light? The answer is found in the previous chapter: 'The glory of God illuminated it, and the Lamb is its light' (Rev. 21:23).

Do you understand what these verses are telling us? There will be no night in heaven, no darkness at all. The shadows of sin and death will all be gloriously removed. There will be no cemeteries in heaven. No funerals, obituary columns or undertakers will be there. There will be no more crying, no more separation and no more sorrow there. But best of all, the church's beloved will be there, resplendent in glory and beautiful as the dawn, and in his light we shall see light

On that day these words from the prophet Zechariah will be gloriously fulfilled:

> And in that day it shall be
> That living waters shall flow from Jerusalem,
> Half of them toward the eastern sea
> And half of them toward the western sea;
> In both summer and winter it shall occur.
> And the LORD shall be King over all the earth.
> In that day it shall be —
> 'The LORD is one,'
> And his name one
>
> (Zech. 14:8).

There will be no summer to dry up the river of life or winter to freeze it over. The life God's people will enjoy on that day will be perfect and permanent, and the knowledge of the glory of God will cover the earth as the waters cover the sea (Hab. 2:14).

Until then

Heed the Word

In his helpful commentary on the Song of Solomon, Stuart Olyott raises an interesting question: 'If you had been writing this love poem, how would you have ended it? Very probably with an idyllic picture of the two lovers together in perfect union, bathing in each other's affection. But the Holy Spirit thought differently. The closing picture is one of separation. The king has gone away, and the bride, filled with longing, cannot wait for him to reappear. The last recorded words of the bride express her deepest wish that the king should make haste to return. The parallel between the end of the Song and the close of the book of Revelation is obvious. The heart of the loving believer cries to his absent Lord, "Come, Lord Jesus." And we shall not be disappointed. Throughout his absence we have in our hands his written promise: "Surely I come quickly!" (Revelation 22:20).'³

The book that contains that written promise is our light in this dark world until the dawning of the eternal day. The apostle Peter calls attention to the light of God's Word by saying, 'We also have the prophetic word made more sure [or confirmed], which you do well to heed as a light that shines in a dark place, until the day dawns and the morning star rises in your hearts' (2 Peter 1:19).

David shared this assessment of the Word of God. He writes, 'Your word is a lamp to my feet and a light to my path' (Ps. 119:105). And Solomon adds, 'For the commandment is a lamp, and the law is light' (Prov. 6:23).

Marvellous as it is to have this light shining in this dark world, it will be of no avail to us, if we refuse to follow Peter's admonition to 'Take heed.' Many refuse to do so. The world is a murky, dingy place. The darkness of sin abounds on every hand. One would think a bright ray of light would be welcomed, but it is not. Scripture tells us that men '[love] darkness rather than light because their deeds [are] evil' (John 3:19).

An old story conveys this truth very well. An Arab sat in his tent with a candle burning. He picked up a fig, broke it open, found a worm and threw it away. He broke open another fig, found another worm and discarded it. The third fig produced a third worm. He picked up a fourth fig, leaned over and blew out the candle! Many blame the light of the Word of God rather than the sin it exposes.

Even though God's people love and embrace the light of God's Word, they too can refuse to take heed to it at various points. When they do, the dinginess of the world filters in and deprives them of the peace and joy that are rightfully theirs.

> Lord, thy Word abideth
> And our footsteps guideth.
> Who its truth believeth
> Light and joy receiveth.

(Henry W. Baker)

Conclusion

18.
The challenge posed by an altogether lovely Christ

We have traversed a lot of ground as we have looked for Christ in the Song of Solomon. It is not difficult to find him there. The difficulty rather is deciding which pictures of him to include. We are gravely mistaken, however, if we make this search for Christ a mere academic pursuit. We look for Christ, not to demonstrate our cleverness in finding him, but to stand in awe before him and to further impress upon our hearts the need to worship and serve him.

The Shulamite's many expressions of love for her beloved test and challenge the child of God at several points. I find, however, that none challenges me more than those two words, 'altogether lovely' (5:16). Although we looked briefly at this expression in a previous chapter, I am compelled to return to it and to listen to these words again. As I do so, I hear four calls to the people of God.

A call to examine

First, if Christ is 'altogether lovely', then he is deserving of our total love. These words, therefore, constrain us to examine our priorities along certain lines.

Careful contemplation

The bride's language is that of careful contemplation. The term
'altogether lovely' is not the language of one who has spent
only a brief moment or two with someone and only casually
observed him during that time. It is rather the language of one
who has walked with a friend and carefully and intently observed him. The overriding lesson here for us is this: if we
would see the loveliness of Jesus Christ, we must make it our
business to study and to meditate upon him.

How seriously we fail in these areas! In his sermon on this
text, Charles Spurgeon traces a failure to discern the loveliness of Christ to ignorance of his person and lack of meditation. He says meditation is 'the most soul-fattening' of all
the things we can do, especially when we combine it with
prayer. He calls the lack of meditation 'a very serious robber
of the wealth of renewed hearts'.[1]

Passionate love

The term 'altogether lovely' also expresses the Shulamite's
passionate love for Solomon. These are not the words of someone who is giving a cool, analytical assessment of another. It
is not the language of one who is detached and removed from
the object of which she is speaking. No! She is personally involved here. Her emotions are stirred. Spurgeon says hers is
'the utterance of a soul that is altogether overcome with admiration... Lost in adoring wonder, the gracious mind desists
from description, and cries with rapture: "Yea, he is altogether
lovely." '[2]

Spurgeon proceeds to apply this to the Christian's view: 'It
has often been thus with true saints; they have felt the love of
Jesus to be overpowering and inebriating. Believers are not
always cool and calm in their thoughts towards their Lord.'[3]

The Shulamite reveals the depth of the love she felt for Solomon in these words:

> Set me as a seal upon your heart,
> As a seal upon your arm;
> For love is as strong as death,
> Jealousy as cruel as the grave;
> Its flames are flames of fire,
> A most vehement flame.
> Many waters cannot quench love,
> Nor can the floods drown it.
> If a man would give for love
> All the wealth of his house,
> It would be utterly despised

(8:6-7).

True love is passionate love. It is as strong as death, consuming all before it. It burns with flames of fire. There is nothing lukewarm or half-hearted about true love. It cannot be drowned, even by the waters of a raging torrent. And it cannot be bought. If a millionaire were to offer all his wealth as an inducement to a person in love to withhold love, that person would laugh at him and go right on loving.

The Shulamite recognized that Solomon loved her with this kind of love and she longed for two things. Firstly, she wanted him to continue to love her with a passionate love. 'Set me as a seal upon your heart, as a seal upon your arm', she begs him. Seals, worn around the neck or on the wrist, were often used as emblems of affection. She wanted to continue to be Solomon's object of special affection. Secondly, the Shulamite expressed her desire to reciprocate his love with a passionate love of her own.

In the same way, the church recognizes that Christ has loved her with a love that is 'as strong as death'. There can be no doubt about this. Christ actually went down into the depths of death because of his love for his church. And that death was like no other death. There on the cross the Lord actually experienced the pangs and anguish of hell itself, so that the wrath of God against his people would be appeased.

Christ's love for the church was so great that nothing could quench it. It burned like fire and all the oceans of the world could not drown it. And it could not be bought. There in the wilderness Satan offered the Lord all the kingdoms of this world if he would only forget about his love for his church (Matt. 4:8-9). But Jesus refused to be bought. Rather, he marched firmly ahead to Calvary's cross, where he bought the church with the ransom price of his own blood.

This is the love Christ had for the church, and because Christ has loved her in such a way, the church desires to love him in that same unquenchable, relentless way, to love him with a love that scorns anything that would diminish it, or carry it away.

A call to be unashamed

Next, the term 'altogether lovely' drives us to this conclusion: we should never be ashamed of Christ.

The young bride was not the least bit ashamed of her beloved, or of her love for him. When the daughters of Jerusalem asked why he was so special to her, she launched into a detailed description of his beauty without the slightest hesitation. She did not mince words. She did not withhold praise from her beloved out of fear that her listeners would think her too lavish with her praise.

Can we, as Christians, identify ourselves with her wholehearted, enthusiastic praise for her beloved? Are we unashamedly proclaiming the virtues and glories of the true Beloved, Christ Jesus?

A call to be like Christ

A third lesson can be drawn from the term 'altogether lovely' as applied to Christ. If we want to be lovely ourselves, we must be like Christ. In other words, the more Christlike we are, the more lovely we shall be.

Is Christ kind and patient? Then we too must strive to be kind and patient. Is Christ forgiving? Then we also must be forgiving. Is Christ pure and holy? Then so must we be. But how is it possible to be like Christ? It would be impossible, were it not for the fact that he has given us his own Holy Spirit to dwell in our hearts and bring forth his fruit in our lives.

Oh, that the desire to be Christlike would seize each of one of us until we could truly sing:

> Let the beauty of Jesus be seen in me,
> All his wonderful passion and purity;
> O thou Spirit divine,
> All my nature refine,
> Till the beauty of Jesus be seen in me!
>
> (Albert Orsborn)

A call to service

A fourth lesson is this: if Christ is altogether lovely, we must eagerly serve him. How many of us are doing so? How many of us regard the slightest act of service as an onerous and burdensome duty? In his sermon on this text, Charles Spurgeon refers to 'those of old' who 'bore poverty and dared reproach, marched weary leagues, passed tempestuous seas, bore perils of robbers and of cruel men, to plant the cross in lands where as yet Jesus was not known'.[4] He further suggests that such labours were considered 'commonplace' in those days but 'nowadays could not be expected'.[5] Then Spurgeon poses a probing and disturbing question: 'Is Christ less lovely, or is his church less loyal?'[6] Is he? Are we?

A call to love others

A final lesson from the loveliness of Christ for us to take to our hearts has to do with loving others. Think about this for a moment. If Christ is altogether lovely, and all believers are 'in him', it must mean there is a loveliness about each and every child of God. If we love Christ, then, we must love our fellow-Christians as well.

The apostle John drives this point home with these telling words: 'If someone says, "I love God," ' and hates his brother, he is a liar; for he who does not love his brother whom he has seen, how can he love God whom he has not seen? And this commandment we have from him: that he who loves God must love his brother also' (1 John 4:20-21).

The term 'altogether lovely' has, then, a practical relevance. We cannot just sit in church and say it or sing it. If we believe Christ is truly lovely, it puts us under an obligation to demonstrate it every day of our lives. The church will do her work at a snail's pace until she convinces the world that her Christ is the most lovely person one can know. And she will convince the world that this is so, only when she firmly believes it herself and lives accordingly.

Notes

Chapter 1 — The fragrance of Christ
1. William Hendriksen, *New Testament Commentary: Matthew,* Baker Book House, p.173.
2. As above.
3. As above, p.172.
4. As above, p.173.
5. Walter Chantry, *Praises for the King of Kings,* The Banner of Truth Trust, p.85.

Chapter 2 — Christ proclaiming his excellence
1. Geoffrey B. Wilson, *Revelation, A Digest of Reformed Comment,* Evangelical Press, p.24.

Chapter 3 — The church proclaims him flawless
1. George Burrowes, *A Commentary on the Song of Solomon,* The Banner of Truth Trust, p.426.
2. Stuart Olyott, *A Life Worth Living and a Lord Worth Loving,* Evangelical Press, p.107.
3. John Flavel, *The Works of John Flavel,* The Banner of Truth Trust, vol. ii, p.215.
4. John Gill, *Exposition of the Old and New Testaments,* The Baptist Standard Bearer, Inc., vol. iv, p.669.
5. Burrowes, *The Song of Solomon,* pp.426-7.

Chapter 4 — The church proclaims his beauty
1. Burrowes, *The Song of Solomon,* p.431.
2. As above, p.432.
3. As above.
4. Olyott, *A Life Worth Living,* p.107.

5. Franz Delitsch, *Commentary on the Song of Songs and Ecclesiastes,* Wm B. Eerdmans Publishing Company, p.106.
6. James Durham, *An Exposition of the Song of Solomon,* The Banner of Truth Trust, p.315.

Chapter 5 — The church proclaims his strength
1. Burrowes, *The Song of Solomon,* p.433.
2. Trent C. Butler, Editor, *Holman Bible Dictionary,* Holman Bible Publishers, p.167.
3. John Gill, *Exposition,* vol. iv, p.672.
4. As above, p.673.
5. Durham, *Exposition of Song of Solomon,* p.299.

Chapter 6 — The kisses of Christ
1. Durham, *Exposition of Song of Solomon*, p.317.
2. Charles Spurgeon, *Metropolitan Tabernacle Pulpit,* Pilgrim Publications, vol. xlii, p.401.
3. Charles Spurgeon, *Treasury of David,* MacDonald Publishing Company, vol. i, p.11.

Chapter 8 — With Christ in the banqueting hall
1. Erroll Hulse, *The Believer's Experience,* Carey Publications, p.165.
2. Matthew Henry, *Matthew Henry's Commentary on the Whole Bible,* vol. iv, p.601.
3. Burrowes, *The Song of Solomon*, p.275.
4. Henry, *Commentary,* vol. iii, p.1063.
5. Olyott, *A Life Worth Living,* p.101.
6. Henry, *Commentary,* vol. iii, p.1063.
7. As above.
8. As above.
9. Martyn Lloyd-Jones, *God's Ultimate Purpose,* Baker Book House, p.276.
10. As above.

Chapter 9 — The gracious voice of Christ
1. W. Robertson Nicoll, *The Expositor's Dictionary of Texts,* Baker Book House, vol. i, part ii, p.561.

Chapter 10 — Declension: Christ's voice spurned
1. Henry, *Commentary,* vol. iii, p.1081.
2. Spurgeon, *Met. Tab. Pulpit,* vol. xiv, p.68.
3. As above, p.71.

Chapter 11 — The friendship of Christ
1. Spurgeon, *Met. Tab. Pulpit,* vol. xix, p.382.
2. Edward D. Griffin, *The Life and Sermons of Edward D. Griffin,* Banner of Truth Trust, vol. ii, p.61.

Chapter 12 — A church made fair
1. Olyott, *A Life Worth Living,* p.117.
2. D. Martyn Lloyd-Jones, *Life in the Spirit,* Baker Book House, p.156.
3. L. Berkhof, *Systematic Theology,* Wm B. Eerdmans Publishing Co., p.532.

Chapter 13 — For Christ alone
1. This version of the hymn is taken from *Grace Hymns,* Grace Publications Trust, no. 458.
2. Quoted by Lloyd-Jones, *Life in the Spirit,* p.167.

Chapter 14 — The church and the gospel
1. Hendriksen, *John,* vol. ii, p.26.
2. Ryle, *Expository Thoughts on the Gospels: John,* vol. ii, p.47.
3. Olyott, *A Life Worth Living,* p.114.
4. As above, p.115.

Chapter 15 — The church triumphant
1. Geoffrey B. Wilson, *Ephesians: A Digest of Reformed Comment,* Banner of Truth Trust, p.130.

Chapter 16 — Christ's love fulfilled
1. John R. W. Stott, *The Bible Speaks Today: The Message of Ephesians,* Inter-Varsity Press, p.56.
2. As above.
3. Wilson, *Ephesians,* p.36.

Chapter 17 — Longing for daybreak
1. Durham, *The Song of Solomon,* p.157.
2. Henry, *Commentary,* vol. iv, p.1469.
3. Olyott, *A Life Worth Living,* pp.120-21.

Chapter 18 — The challenge posed by an altogether lovely Christ
1. Spurgeon, *Met. Tab. Pulpit,* vol. xvii, p.400.
2. As above, p.399.
3. As above.
4. As above, p.405.
5. As above.
6. As above.